About The Author

Robert Spence is a popular sales trainer, sales coach, speaker, author and self-confessed 'Sales Nerd'.

Having worked in sales for almost all of his adult life, Robert founded Paragon Sales Solutions; a leading sales and and marketing consultancy firm set up with the sole intention to help businesses and individuals do better with their sales and marketing.

Robert has also authored 'Relationship Selling' and 'The Paragon Mindset'; two top selling sales books available to buy on Amazon.

As the MD of Paragon, Sales Director of Stones Events and Sales Director of Incite Video, Robert's main intentions and focus is to constantly drive sales forward whilst never forgetting the importance of customer focus and care.

Now, you might be wondering why Robert has gone on to author yet another amazing sales book! Well, the answer is quite simple: Robert sees sales as an ever growing and developing skill set that so few are taught. By investing in books like this, and his others, you are investing in yourself, your career and your future.

This book will also act as a guide for Robert's future online course to further help your understanding of the sales process and sales psychology.

You are more than welcome to contact Robert directly;

paragonsalessolutions.co.uk

T: @robjohnspence
Insta: @robjohnspence

A Month to Improve Your Sales

Robert Spence

Copyright © Robert Spence 2019

All Rights Reserved

ISBN: 9798627522364

We all love to sell.

It creates a thrill, a rush and a sense of achievement that is unrivalled.

Some of us are born with a natural ability to sell.

Others need to work hard to set up a strong sales skill set.

If you own a business, this book will help you to sell more.

If you are a sales professional, this book will help you to sell more.

If you are an entrepreneur, this book will help you to sell more.

Ultimately, this book was written to help you to improve your sales within a month.

Shall we make a start?

Robert Spence
March 2019

www.improveyoursales.co.uk

A Month to Improve Your Sales	9
Question Everything	13
The Gatekeeper	22
Social Selling	29
Main Objections	38
Sales Call Reluctance	48
Handling Rejection	54
Public Speaking	61
Everyone's a Customer	67
Unbeatable Telesales	72
What to do When Sales are Down	79
Don't Discount; Add Value	85
Making the Most of Networking	91
Using Your Voice	98
The Bigger Picture	104
Consultative Selling	108
The Need to Follow Up	115
List Objections Early	122
What are you Selling?	126
Captivate Your Audience	131
Handling Your Competition	137
Keep Prospecting	142
Staying Healthy	150
Owning up to Mistakes	159
Buying Signals	164
Developing Rapport	169
The Test Close	175
Understand Your Sales Process	182
Managing Expectations	187
Hitting Your Sales Target	190
Don't Close the Sale!	193
Closing the Sale	198
Your Next Steps	207
Other Works by Robert Spence	211

A Month to Improve Your Sales

I am a firm believer in the fact that to make a business succeed you need to sell - and you need to sell well.

I have seen companies with a poor product do incredibly well due to their solid, proactive and dedicated sales team. And I have also seen businesses with an unbeatable and unrivalled product go under because sales processes and skill sets were not put into good use from the very start; and weren't worked on when things started to go wrong.

The ability to sell, and having the confidence and skill set to sell is needed now more than ever. Sure, we are moving towards a digital age where every Tom, Dick and Harry can preach about the need to 'automate' sales, and people are starting to look at creating marketing models that take away the need for sales people. But let's face it; these techniques and models are just fads that will soon die out.

There has always been a need for sales professionals, and there always will be.

And that is one of the many reasons why I have decided to sit down and write this book.

I am a firm believer that good quality sales skills not only need to be taught, they also need to be practiced, rehearsed and revised. Sales skills are just like any other form of skill; if you are not going to practice them then you will only lose them over time. But also the learning of new skills should be fun, interesting and not time consuming.

And let's not hide from the fact that everybody is a sales person. I don't care if you work in sales or not; there will be times in your life where you have to persuade someone of something, or have to negotiate some form of deal or plan. If you are a buyer for a large company, there will be times in your life when you have to 'sell' the idea of a cheaper deal with your supplier, or even a shorter delivery schedule. If you are a teenager, you might need to 'sell' to your parents that you need to stay up later than normal. If you are an entrepreneur, of course your life will be FULL of sales opportunities. Hell, even if you are just trying to negotiate a discount on the next car you buy you are still trying to 'sell' the idea that you deserve it at a cheaper rate than the list price.

Of course, most likely the reason you are reading this book is because you work in sales, own a business or are an entrepreneur and you are trying to improve your sales skills.

One of my main concerns with the sales industry is that it is unregulated, and would always be very hard, if not impossible, to regulate. You see, working in sales can be relatively easy. Sales jobs are always available and can be picked up by anyone with no qualifications and also little experience. Although there are of course plenty of advantages to this, it also leaves sales people at a loss as how to progress in their career. Sure, if you keep doing well and you keep closing lots of sales then you will find yourself up for promotion relatively quickly. But what happens to people who are finding it tough in sales? They leave, they quit, or they turn to more deceitful tactics to close more sales; such as simple manipulation tricks, high pressure, and sometimes lying. That is where self-education comes into play.

Having worked in sales for the majority of my adult life, and having worked alongside and learned from some of the best sales professionals around, I can tell you that one of the best ways to learn about sales techniques is through reading inspirational and motivational sales guides - just like this. A quick browse on Amazon or other leading book stores will give you access to thousands upon thousands of sales guides all of which have been written by top sales people. But as a business owner, entrepreneur or career professional, do you have time to sit through a manuscript that beats around the bush without giving you solid answers? I am sure you don't!

That is why this book has been written and designed to offer you the chance to read just a short, quick and concise chapter every single day. I don't want to bore you with chapter after chapter of boring content that leads nowhere. Nor do I want to preach to you about how I am the greatest sales person of all time and you should listen to me waffle on about my successes and you should bow down to me and learn from my business and sales lessons (I am joking of course).

This is a book full of valuable tips that you can digest in next to no time at all - most likely 15 minutes per day.

There are 31 chapters in this book, one for every day of the month; just don't read it in February! Read just a short chapter every single day and I guarantee that you will improve your sales profoundly. To be fair, there is no exact order to this book either; you could in theory read each chapter in any order - there is nothing stopping you! But just get ready to have plenty of red-hot sales knowledge, tips and advice fired at you for every day of the month and get ready to see your sales increase, your career excel and ultimately see your business thrive.

Whether you are reading this as a sales professional, a business owner, or because I pressured you into reading this book as a friend - this book will change your sales, your career, and your business for the better!

Question Everything

This first chapter is going to be an absolute game changer for you. In fact, I really feel that the majority of the points I am to make in this chapter will be the most beneficial points throughout the whole book and will make for a good foundation moving forward.

Over the past several years, I have had the pleasure of working alongside, coaching and learning from some of the greatest sales people and business owners this Country has to offer. This has allowed me to watch, observe and take notes on the skills that these people possess and put into action.

To narrow down one skill that separates a great sales professional from an average sales person is very tough - however one skill really stands out, and can make a total difference to a person's selling ability. What is that skill I hear you ask?

Questioning

The ability to question your prospect or your potential customer is what is truly going to help you see an increase in your sales.

I see it like this; the best sales people in the world see themselves as detectives, or even to some degree they see themselves as doctors. Let's stick to the doctor analogy as this is always a nice and easy way to explain my reasonings.

What happened the last time you felt unwell enough to go and see the doctor? I would assume you didn't walk in, sit down and have the doctor take one look at you and say:

"Ahh yes, you are going to need some antibiotics!"

Of course that would not happen. The likelihood of the matter is that the doctor would have greeted you, sat you down and asked you;

"So, what seems to be the problem?" Or, "How can I help you today?"

From there, you will have gone on to describe your symptoms in as much detail as you can. The doctor will sit and listen, and then go on to ask more questions;

"Ok. And how long has it been like this? Have you felt this way before? Have you noticed any other symptoms? Do you, or any of your family members have a history of these symptoms?"

From this line of questioning, the doctor will be able to diagnose the issue or the problem, and prescribe some form of medication or solution to your problem.

If you follow this same frame of mind as a sales person, normally you will quite easily discover exactly what your customer needs. And once you have discovered what your customer needs, you can then go on to 'prescribe' your product or service and offer something that your prospect simply cannot turn down.

Sales people are merely just problem solvers when it boils down to it!

It sounds so simple, right? But honestly, it truly is that simple. By sitting back and asking your prospect the right questions there does not need to be any 'hardcore closing' or manipulative sales techniques put to use. You just need to ask the right kind of questions, and then once your potential customer reveals what they are looking for or the kinds of problems they are facing, all you then need to do is sell them your solution.

In your line of work, and in your past history of making presentations and proposals; do you feel you asked enough questions? Or did you just try to talk over your prospect and sell them what you felt suited them, and tried to sell them what *you* wanted to sell? Instead of selling them something *they* want to buy?

Nine times out of ten, if you are able to use some good questioning and sit back and listen to your prospect you will ultimately allow the prospect to sell the product or service to themselves without too much effort or suggestion from yourself. And not only that, but you will develop a strong and solid relationship with your customer; at the end of the day, we never liked to be talked to, or pitched to. But we love to have a conversation.

This then brings me on to my next point; open and closed questions. It is important at this stage to understand the difference between these two types of questions, and how you too can use them to your advantage.

If you are new to these terms, allow me to quickly and briefly explain:

Closed questions are questions that are asked to ensure either a 'yes' or 'no' response is given, or perhaps only a strict choice of answers is offered.

An open question on the other hand relates to a question in which the answer will require slightly more thought and will be more than just a one word answer. Let's think of some quick examples of both just to make it all a bit clearer:

Closed Questions:

- Would you like that in red?
- Is that your final answer?
- Is he dead?

Open Questions:

- What colour would you like that in?
- What are you thoughts on that?
- How do you feel about it all?

You can see that closed questions tend to lead to a one word, short answer whereas an open question can lead to a long, thought of, in-depth answer.

In sales, for years, poorly trained people have tried to use closed questions to push customers into making buying decisions that they potentially may not want to make. It became a form of basic manipulation that so many sales people prided themselves on, however in using them gave sales as an industry a bad name. I had an experience of it recently myself.

A local sports team had approached me to discuss sponsorship opportunities and to discuss what could be on offer for Paragon Sales Solutions. We met, and the meeting went very well in my eyes. For all intents and purposes, I enjoyed the meeting and could certainly see the benefits that a sponsorship agreement could bring for my business. A couple of days later, this person called me up to see if I was in a position to sign up to one of the sponsorship/advertising opportunities that were on offer. Whilst we were talking, without any form of warning, this person immediately asked me:

"So which package would you like to sign up to: the £1500 package, or the £1250 package?"

I was gobsmacked. This is a prime example of a closed question being used badly. Just to put into context, at this stage I hadn't given any indication that I was interested, nor was I given a chance to ask any questions about the deal or the proposal. I responded;

"Well, I have not said that I want to go ahead with a package at all. I think it is best I go away and think about this and I will come back to you."

Eventually I walked away from the deal because I felt pushed and forced into a situation that I didn't really want to be a part of, and unfortunately I have never heard from this individual or the club again.

Has this ever happened to you when you have been trying to buy something?

Here is the thing with closed questions; they can really put your customers backs up. Closed questions may have worked in the 1970s and 1980s when people were selling uPVC windows and conservatories like they were going out of fashion, however we are moving towards a more ethical age of selling in which sales people need to be more like consultants; willing to help, support and problem solve for their customers. Not only that, but the average consumer is well aware of these tactics nowadays and it can be quite insulting to the consumer. The consumer (and when I say that, I mean people like you or I) have been sold to on so many occasions we know what to look out for, and know how to stand our ground.

It is in my professional and personal opinion that when you start to engage with a customer open questions always work better. They allow for a conversation with the customer. They open up a more meaningful, exciting and thrilling conversation that can lead anywhere and everywhere. Sure, some may argue that by asking open questions you put too much 'power' in the hands of the prospect but to me; this is the better place to be.

I always want my customers to be in control and I want my customers to be leading the conversation. As a sales person, my job is to support and help the customer; not to sell to them. I am a problem solver.

Just imagine how the earlier example would have gone if the club owner had asked me:

"Rob, were there any packages that appealed to you?" or "which of the packages do you think would benefit your business the most?"

I would have been a lot more engaging and will have been willing to talk a little more about my needs as a business owner and I am sure we could have come away with the right package for us both.

So, if you are ever tempted to use closed questions to lead, manipulate and control your prospect; don't! You may find out that you are only pushing your customer away to a place where your competitor will sweep them up and take them away from you for good.

Next time you are heading into a sales meeting, or are looking to engage with someone over the phone for the first time, do not be afraid to ask more questions. In doing so, you can easily unearth so many clues as to what your potential customer wants and needs from you, and the pain points they are currently going through.

You are a detective. A doctor. A problem solver.

From here, all you have to do is sit back, advise the customer on what you have to offer and how you can help and once you ask for the sale it should be plain sailing.

The 'Gatekeeper'

Ahhh, the Gatekeeper.

The mythically-named person that fills many a sales person full of dread and fear. The true power force on the opposite end of the phone. The scary person that will never let you speak to the decision maker. The person we must try to 'get past' or 'bypass' - but does it really have to be that way?

Before we go on, let's back track just ever so slightly. Who on earth is this Gatekeeper? What on Earth am I talking about?

The gatekeeper, in effect, is the person stopping you as a sales person from talking to the main decision maker/s and acts as a sort of buffer or barrier to protect the people in charge and the people that make the real buying decisions. Normally, the gatekeeper will be the first person you speak to when you cold call a business, or will be the first person you come into contact with when you walk into an office for the first time.

For years, sales people have feared the gatekeepers of the world. Some, have even admitted to hating gatekeepers. Even now, I have requests from people weekly asking me:

"Rob, how do I get past the gatekeeper?" or, "look, my sales team need help trying to get around the gatekeeper." or even, "I need a sales script that will help me to bypass the gatekeeper and speak directly with the decision maker."

Now, here is the main point, and the main point to this chapter:

If you try to 'get around' the gatekeeper, you are certainly not going to get anywhere fast.

There are a lot of sales professionals, and even sales trainers out there whom pride themselves on their ability to lie, cheat and manipulate their way past the person on the other end of the phone; and this certainly does not sit right with me.

I am a firm believe that the gatekeeper is just as important, and sometimes more important, than the main decision maker themselves. Firstly, we have to remember that the gatekeeper is not some Hagrid style character put there to guard an ancient temple, or a security guard put in place to stop horrible sales people like you from getting through. Gatekeepers are human beings. Just like you and I. They have feelings. Emotions. They go to the toilet. They like to have conversations. They want to feel valued. They want to be respected. Do you think that any human being will feel good, valued and respected if you try to deceive them, manipulate them or undervalue their role within a company? Of course they won't!

It is important to remember that any person entrusted to act as a form of gatekeeper is someone that the company respects and values. This is quite a high powered role, and can entail great power too. If you try to undermine this authority and show disrespect you are going to lose a lot of respect for yourself down the line.

So instead of trying to get around the person taking the call, why don't you try to have a conversation with them instead? Spend time getting to know them. Allow them to be a part of the sales process. The more time you invest with this highly influential person the greater chance you will have of speaking to the decision maker, but they can act as your internal sales person too if you treat them with respect.

I want to talk to you about McDonalds for just a second. We all know the big fast food chain; you cannot drive two miles down the road without seeing the golden arches illuminating the skyline in the distance. Who do you think McDonalds ideal target audience is? No, it's not you! It is your children! McDonalds recognise that their ideal customers are children; which in theory means you are the gatekeeper; Ronald McDonald must get you on side to ultimately get to your children. So as you are driving along, and that big yellow M shines on the horizon your kids shout as they fantasise about the latest Happy Meal toys and heavily processed burgers:

"Mummy, Daddy; can we have a McDonalds?!"

You don't want to cave in and give your kids what they want. But then you start to think about their coffees. You start to picture their sizzling burgers and juicy nuggets dipped in the sweetest of sauces. You can literally taste the McFlurry melting on your tongue. So, you give in to temptation. You pull over, and treat the family to a McDonalds whilst Ronald stares at you, rubbing his hands together with dollar signs in his eyes.

We can look at this scenario in two ways; if McDonalds was a restaurant aimed JUST at kids, would you want to go in? And if it was a restaurant aimed JUST at adults, would your kids want to eat there? The whole branding and ethos within McDonalds is to appeal to a wider audience and to sell to the multiple levels of your family - no matter who the real decision makers are. And you should too within your business or within your sales process.

I am a firm believer, as you might guess from my first book, Relationship Selling, that relationships within a sales cycle are the most important thing you should aim to develop and nurture. But this isn't just with the decision makers; it is with the person on the end of the phone too, or the person that opens the door to you. This goes for the cleaner on a temporary contract too in my eyes.

If you can get someone on side to help you sell, wouldn't your life become easier?

But how do you get the gatekeeper on side? How do you engage with an individual enough so that they allow you five minutes with the decision maker?

Respect

As we discussed earlier, the person picking up the phone, or the first person you bump into at an office is a human being. Respect them. Talk to them. Have a normal conversation no different to how you would the main decision maker. Hell, treat them as if they are the main decision maker (after all, you don't know whether you are already speaking to the main decision maker anyway!) Don't degrade anyone, and don't ever just try to 'get around them'. Sure, they may not be the right person to speak to right now, however get them on side and they can literally walk you into the right office and pull out a chair for you to sit at the main table.

Be Grateful

Manners cost nothing, but can earn you the Earth.

If the person who picks up the phone decides to put you through to the right person; say thank you. If they provide an email address; say thank you. If they tell you the person you are seeking isn't available; say thank you. Now is the time to prove to this company that you are worth doing business with. Think of the bigger picture;

let's say you win the deal or the contract and you walk in and introduce yourself to this person; how do you want me remembered?

Give a Gift

Nine times out of ten if a sales goes through, the gatekeeper will have had some responsibility or had some say in it. This can be from putting you through to the right person, providing you with some great information, or putting a good word in for you behind the scenes. If this is the case, give a gift as a way of saying thank you. It can be a card, a bunch of flowers, a CD, or gift voucher. Or whatever; when you are talking with them find out what they like and enjoy, listen for clues, and give a gift they will truly want and will always remember you for.

Don't Decline a Message

If the person on the end of the phone asks if you would like to leave a message for the person you are trying to reach, be sure to do so! This proves that you trust this person enough to take instructions and that you feel they are good enough at their job to pass the message on. This will solidify the relationship between yourself and the gatekeeper and will build a strong working foundation moving forward. If you treat the conversation well, it will also give you a great chance to have a conversation with the person taking the message.

Insider Treatment

As we mentioned earlier, treating the gatekeeper just as you would the main decision maker can work wonders down the line. Normally a gatekeeper can play a massive influence on the decision maker on your behalf. Let's look at two scenarios; let's pretend you call up Spence Incorporated as a representative of Paragon Sales Solutions and you act rude, abrasive and arrogant towards the call taker. What do you think would happen later on in a conversation over a cup of coffee?

"Oh Joe; I had someone call up from Paragon, I think that's what they were called. He was so awful! Wouldn't let me talk, would not listen to me and was just damn rude! I told him where to go!"

Or, what would happen if you were to call up and treat that call taker like a normal human being:

"Hey Joe! I spoke with Max from Paragon Sales Solutions earlier, can you call him later? Remember how you told me we keep wasting money on XYZ? Well I really think he might be able to help us to save money and streamline our operations."

So, moving forward, do not treat the person on the other end of the phone as an obstacle to get around, or to get through. Think of them as another human being as part of the decision making process and see what happens!

The 'Gatekeeper' is far better on your side, than against it

Social Selling

The way in which we sell is changing near enough by the day. In fact, the way in which we buy, communicate and live our lives is changing much faster now than ever before.

The introduction of the digital age has completely transformed the way in which we go about our daily lives. No longer do we need to write out a shopping list on the back of an old envelope; we can either write down what we need on our phone on a simple note application, or better than that, we can buy exactly what we need from the comfort of our own living room. And with voice operated devices becoming more and more popular all we have to do is walk into a room and say; "Hey Alexa, order me a potato peeler", and lo and behold, one arrives the very next day.

The way us humans communicate and socialise has changed dramatically too. Social media platforms such as Instagram, Facebook, LinkedIn, Twitter and Snapchat have allowed us to stay connected with those people that in the past we may have lose touch with - and I shall leave it up to you to decide if this is a good or a bad thing.

What social media has given us however is the chance for us to be, in theory, more social. More connected. It gives us 24 hour access to people that before we may have only been able to spend two minutes with at a networking event, or a chance encounter at the shop. Of course, social media was never put together to give us sales professionals another opportunity to market our products and to sell, however over time all of the social media channels have adapted to this, and more and more people are turning to social media to sell and to do business.

This in turn has then led to the term 'social selling' to be created.

Now, in the past I have been fairly critical of social selling, and those that have jumped on the bandwagon a little and turned themselves into social selling 'gurus'. And I will come on to that shortly. However it is key to note that it is important that you as a sales professional or business owner utilise social media as another tool in your sales armoury to help you to improve your sales figures.

Let me quickly open up to you about my slight dislike towards the terminology of social selling. Now, social selling is not anything new - it has just adapted itself slightly for this new digital world we live in. However, as social selling itself became more and more popular, it allowed for certain sales people to become lazy. It also allowed some sales professionals to get lucky; many have used social media alone to sell more and have then gone on to preach to people like you and I about how social media and social selling is all you need to sell, and that you can easily hit all of your sales targets just by sending out some emails, writing some blogs, and sliding into some DM's (direct messages).

Of course you can most certainly increase your sales by using social media wisely and by developing relationships with your customers and your audiences however it isn't the holy grail or the saviour of sales. Don't just write one blog post, or send out some connection requests on LinkedIn and expect to become a millionaire from the comfort of your own home. Social selling is merely another tool to your sales toolkit.

Don't put all of your sales and marketing eggs into one basket!

In this chapter, I want to share with you the theories behind social selling, and how you can use social media platforms to sell more. But also allow me to share with you some warnings that you must take note of!

The fact of the matter is this; social selling does work. And used in the right ways can help you to improve your sales dramatically.

One of the key fundamental ideas and reasons you should use social media is that these platforms allow you to get your personal brand out there. Your own personal identity.

I am not talking about your company's brand, or your business' brand, I am talking about YOUR brand. We will talk more about this later, however it is important to remember the fact that people buy from people. The likelihood is that during a sales conversation your customer will buy into YOU more than they will buy into your product or service or business. Your personal brand allows you to market yourself as the incredible, experienced, intelligent and wonderful person that you are. By using social media to put your personal brand out there allows your potential customers and potential buyers to learn more about you and to connect with you on a more personal level.

Years ago as a sales manager for a large company, I did the very same thing. This company had their own social media channels, however I set up my own for the sole purpose of connecting with my customers, to develop and nurture relationships with these people, listening to their needs and to help promote the business I was working for. Before long, my social media presence grew at a rapid pace; not because I was the main brand, but because I was a human being and a person. I was getting more interaction on my channels than the official company channels and I had ultimately become the face and the brand of the company. I was using my own networks to share good news, to listen to gripes and complaints, to find new business and to ultimately be social with the people that I wanted to do business with. And it worked. It worked very well, and not just in tangible results. If I could count the amount of sales and money I made directly on social media it would most likely have been £0. However the relationships I developed eventually led to sales and long-term business agreements.

You can do the same thing too.

According to research published in 2016 by the Aberdeen Group, 72.6% of sales professionals who used social selling as part of their sales process outperformed their sales peers. A recent survey by CSO Insights and Seismic suggested that 31% of B2B sales professionals said that social selling allowed them to build deeper relationships with their clients, and according to Curalate, 50% of consumers say that seeing user-generated content would increase their chances of buying products through a brand's social media.

As you can see, there is plenty of scope here for you to use social networks to your advantage.

However, one word of warning to you; do not just use social selling to, well, sell!

I cannot stand those companies or individuals that just shout; "buy from me, buy from me!" at the top of their lungs on social media - it puts the audiences off and if you start to do this it will actually have more of a detrimental effect on your sales performance. Have you ever received a connection request on LinkedIn, accepted it, to then only have a message from that person within seconds telling you what they do, why they are so good, and why you should buy from them? It is embarrassing, right? My rule is this; if you would not act like it in person, or at a networking event, don't do it online!

Social media is no different to the real world; don't act weird!

Being alert on social media and social platforms allows you to prospect in ways that have been hard to do before. Not only can you connect with people who may have a need for your product or service, by using some cunning detective skills you can easily search for people actually looking for what you offer within the click of the button. As social media has connected all of us from every corner of the globe, even motivated buyers are taking to social media to look out for recommendations from their peers, connections and friends - this is the perfect opportunity for you to keep your eyes on the radar and swoop in when the opportunity arises. I am not encouraging you to spend all day every day just refreshing your searches to find people whom you can sell to, but be sure to use social media as another tool in your selling tool kit that you can use as and when you need it. As we will discuss later on in the book, a full sales pipeline at times is more important than the actual closing of sales and so if you can use social media as a way to keep that sales pipeline full then it will be sure to pay dividends over time.

You will hear me bang on about this quite a lot in this book, and for good reason too, but relationships are crucial when it comes to selling. We buy from people we like. We go back to the people we like. We refer others to people we like. So if you can develop strong relationships with people, then over time you will see your sales go through the roof! By remaining SOCIAL on social media you will get the chance to improve your relationships with people. It will give you the chance to get to know your potential customers and also gives them the chance to get to know you too. Don't be too fake about it however. I have seen too many dodgy social media 'trainers' and 'gurus' talk about the need to congratulate others and to leave comments on posts etc. Which yes, I agree with completely - however make sure you remain genuine. If you are just saying, 'great post!' or 'thanks for sharing' to just brown nose then you just come across as a desperate suck ass who needs to learn how to converse with other human beings. Once again, if you would not say it in person, or would word things a certain or different way in person, be sure to do it that same way online too. If you see a post by someone and you like it, be sure to comment on it and 'like' it - however ensure you are genuine about it and you haven't just copy and pasted the comment or used an autofill comment that some social media platforms use.

Always be sure to bring the virtual to the reality also. One thing that I find truly benefits me with social media is that I can bring up certain posts and events when I next see that person in the real world! Simple comments can really go a long way, and show that you do care, and that you do pay attention:

"Hey! How was that event you went to last night?" or "Congratulations on that award the other week - how was the events evening?"

If you play the social selling card really well, you can soon become the expert in your field. The 'go-to' person. The person that everyone refers to when faced with certain problems. You can do this in any field, whether you are a marketer, an accountant, a fencing coach, a hairdresser and even a bespoke desk builder. If you can become the expert in your chosen field, your potential customers will come to you; hence why putting across your personal brand will certainly go a very long way.

To make this happen you need to use social media to stand yourself apart. Write blog posts and articles about your chosen expertise. Tweet and post regularly about it. Engage positively with conversations. Host live video webinars about the subject. Do all you can to niche your offering down and set yourself as the person that is so passionate and dedicated to your industry that your potential customer will be mad to go anywhere else!

Want the upper hand when it comes to social selling? Keep notes on all of the opportunities that you have created and notes on the conversations you have had; this is where a good CRM (Customer Relationship Management system) comes into play. Of course you do not want to blind your sales manager with false opportunities or fill it up with things that might not happen. But if you have had a solid conversation that has even the slightest chance of going anywhere then make a note. This will allow you the chance to follow up on these lead no differently to how you would a normal enquiry, even if it just needs to be followed up in the long-term.

Finally, before we move on, one word of warning. Do not

allow social selling to over take your life and allow you to become lazy with your sales cycle. Unfortunately, I am seeing a trend, particularly within the younger audience of sales professionals who would much prefer to send an email or a message to follow up, or will literally not pick up the phone and will try every other form of electronic contact they can to get out of having a real conversation. Limit your time on social media. Social media can be quite dangerous and despite your good intentions to go online to find your next customer and to engage in a few conversations you can easily find yourself looking at Game of Throne spoilers, photos of your ex, and highlights of the last football game. Limit your time, don't start to procrastinate and set yourself some targets as to why you are online and what you aim to achieve and you will come out on top.

Main Objections

No matter what you are selling, and no matter how accomplished of a sales person you are, you will always face some objections of some variety. Some people class them as rebuttals, some class them as rejections; but ultimately it is very rare that you will pitch whatever it is you are selling without hearing some form of objection.

We all face objections. It is how we handle them that stands the best apart from the rest.

Don't worry; every single one of us sales people and business owners will hear or face objections of some form or another. But the trick here is to understand what objections are, why the occur, and what you can do to overcome them.

Have you ever heard of any of the following?

"I need to think about it."
"I don't have the money right now."
"I need to speak with my partner."
"Yeah it does sound good, I think for now I just need to carry on as I am and see how things turn out."
"It sounds far too expensive to me."

All of these are the most common objections any of us are ever going to face. Sure, they may come in different guises or might be worded ever so slightly differently - but let's face it, we have all heard at least one of these at some stage in our lives.

Right now, I want to look at the essence behind these objections; the basic psychology behind them so that we can develop a strong understanding for the chapters to come. We will also look at some simple tips and ideas that you can use whenever you are faced with one of these objections.

These objections can relate to anything you are selling whether it be face to face, over the phone, even in your marketing strategies online too.

I believe it was Zig Ziglar whom first mentioned that there are really only five main reasons why your customer will not buy from you:

- No Money
- No Need
- No Desire
- No Hurry
- No Trust

For me, these five points work as umbrellas for any other objections you may hear and you can probably categorise any objections into these five. And also, I would say that one out of all of these five is the most important objection that can hold the rest together - but we will come on to that shortly.

Allow me to break these objections down a little more so we can understand them in way more detail!

No Money

Of course, a lot of what we buy, or decide not to buy stems down to money - or sometimes, a lack of. No matter what anyone tries to say, money does make the world go around. People work hard for their money and rightfully so they want to keep a check on how it is spent. You may hear responses such as:

"I can't afford it."
"Sorry, it is just way out of my budget."
"I cannot justify the cost right now."

Sometimes, trying to get over the fact your prospect does not have the budget is tough. If they cannot afford it, then what can you do?

The money objection does have some simple hacks however to work around if you are willing to work hard and ask the right questions and come up with the right solutions.

One key trick is to ensure you have completely sold the value of what it is you are offering (we will go through this in more detail later on in the book). But have you informed your customer about the extra value your product or service can offer? The money it can help them save? The benefits it can help bring to them or their company? Sometimes people are willing to pay more if it means they know they will receive a high-level of customer service, or if they know they will get long-term support and guidance.

Also, with the right questioning, can you find out if they can't afford your product or service in general, or if they cannot afford it in one chunk? Whether you are selling B2B (business to business) or B2C (business to consumer), cashflow can be a real issue and the ability to pay for something in a large chunk can be tough. Can you offer any payment plans? Can you organise a good breakdown in fees? Or with the right questioning, can you look to speak to the prospect again when they have set out their budgets for the next quarter?

No Need

There is nothing worse than having a sleazy salesperson trying to sell us something that we simply do not have a need for.

There will come a time when you try to engage with a prospect that does not want or need your product or service. The key to this however is to ensure that you question your prospect in detail way before you ever get to the closing stage. Why waste your valuable time trying to sell to someone who doesn't need what you are selling?

Would it not be better to stop the sales pitch or sales conversation on the first hint that the customer mentions that there is no need, and to ask your prospect if they know anyone that would have a need for your services?

Gone are the days in which a 'hardcore closer' or slick tongued sales person can persuade someone to buying something they do not need. The general public are so accustomed to sales manipulation techniques that a short term sale can incur greater issues down the line; buyers remorse, returns, complaints, bad reviews etc. Is this really what you want?

So be sure to go back to Chapter 1 and think about your questioning techniques. Ask the right questions and you will stop wasting your precious time on people whom simply do not need your product or service and focus on those that do.

No Desire

I am a massive fan of emotions. Emotions are what make us humans tick. Without emotions, what do we become?

This is why I always urge business owners to keep some form of human contact with their customers. In this modern age it is so easy to set up some crazy automated marketing funnel and to drip-feed emails and to automate everything; but they do not contain emotional connections - and it is emotional connections that generate desire.

Look at life this way; we never want to pay money for our water bill, do we? When we have to pay money for something we need, there is some form of resentment towards it. This could be car insurance, a gas bill or even your TV license. None of us like paying for those things, do we? And yet we need them.

But what happens when we see something that we desire? The latest iPhone perhaps? A stunning pair of shoes? The latest Playstation game? We don't mind paying over the odds for these items because there is an emotional attachment there. There is a sense of desire there. And this desire stems from emotion.

If you can build up an emotional bond between your prospect and your product or service then their desire to own it, to possess it, or to use it grows.

This is why you are encouraged to take cars out on test drives; you can then picture yourself driving the car and parking it on your drive after a long hard day at work. This is why businesses like Netflix give you a free trial. You, as the consumer get the chance to try it out, get used to it, ultimately fall in love with it and then you cannot see your life without it; leading you to buy it!

In your sales pitch, use emotive language to engage your customer and to build their desire up. Get them to imagine using your product or service. Describe in detail how much better their life would be with whatever it is you are selling. Allow them to touch, taste, smell, and use your product and give them the chance to fall in love with it. There is nothing wrong with using pure, real emotion to sell.

No Hurry

Did you know that some websites now have automatic countdown timers stating that their sale will end within a set amount of time, and yet if you go on the website the next day, the timer starts afresh?

Have you ever walked into a shop to see signs saying; 'sale must end today!' or 'all stock must go'?

Both of these simple techniques encourage a sense of urgency for your prospect to make a decision, and to make a purchase sooner rather than later.

The fact of the matter is that urgency does work, and it removes the chance for your prospect to walk away and 'think about it'.

There are ways to create urgency with any product or service and it is up to your creative mind to find one that works.

It could be simply limiting the spaces on your course to

ensure that people want to book before it is too late. It could be running a special promotion that allows the next three carpet cleans to come with a free oven clean too. It could be the suggestion that the item is low in stock and you don't know when it will be back in.

Even Big Issue sellers like to incur a sense of urgency, and a sense of scarcity. How many times have you walked past a Big Issue seller trying to sell their 'last copy' so that they can finish for the day, only to discover that they have a stash hidden elsewhere.

If you can find a way to hurry a prospect into making a purchase you are going to see a reduction in the amount of people stating they need to think about a decision, or need to speak with their partners; if the offer is so good to refuse they will bite your hand off and think of the consequences further down the line.

No Trust

Out of all the categories of objections you will ever face, the 'no trust' objection is the biggest, and most common objection you will face.

Let's face it, we are bombarded with messages left right and centre from advertisers and marketers all wanting our hard-earned money. We are also hearing stories on a daily basis of people who have lost money to scam artists and to products or services that never came came as promised or as described.

This has put many consumers and businesses on the back foot; we simply do not know who to trust. And this means that we will either not buy full stop, or we will only stick with our current suppliers or people we know.

So the need to develop trust is key to any sales process. Relationships develop trust quicker than any other form of selling. Your potential customer wants to know that you are not just going to take their money and run, and that you aren't just going to rip them off, or under deliver on your promises.

Trust does take time, and trust does take patience, but if you are willing to work hard then trust can be developed and worked on. It could be a case of always sticking with your word, allowing your prospect time to digest your customer testimonials, it could mean that the sales process takes a little longer so that your prospect can get to know you and your business in more detail - but eventually it will pay off.

I am a firm believer that many people will use one of the other objections we have mentioned as a cover up for the fact they do not trust you. It is rare to find someone so upfront and honest that they say, "Yeah, I don't want to buy this because I don't trust you." It is far easier and safer for your prospect to blame their decision on their budget, or to suggest that they need to think about. That is why your ability to develop a relationship, and develop a sense of trust with your prospect will pay dividends down the line.

Later on in this book we are going to look at ways you can overcome these objections and some good techniques you can use to ensure that an objection never holds you back again!

Sales Call Reluctance

Apart from face to face selling, nothing beats a good sales call. Selling over the phone is still one of the greatest things you can do to sell your product or your service. It ultimately is the biggest disruptive form of marketing there is, and by engaging your potential customer in a real conversation you will see a higher rate of success. Sure, social media marketing and social selling is effective and should not be overlooked, but the telephone truly is a wonderful tool.

An email can be ignored, but can a ringing telephone?

Not only that, but the phone call allows you to develop a better relationship with your prospect and will give you the chance to get across your message in a much better and concise manner.

According to statistics published by Hubspot, only 24% of sales emails are ever opened - just less than a quarter! Hence why the telephone is so effective. And to underline the importance of the phone ever further, Professor Albery Mehrabian of the University of California, LA, published his studies in the 1970's that suggested that we deduce our feelings, attitudes and beliefs about what someone says not by the actual words spoken, but by the speaker's body language and tone of voice; and to quantify these statistics, they look like 7% for words spoken, 38% on body language and 55% for tone of voice when it comes to personal communication. On the telephone, you of course cannot portray your body language, but your tone of voice will come across perfectly.

That's why you should still pick up the phone!

However, from time to time even the best sales people out there suffer from what is known as 'sales call reluctance'. Think of this as the inability to pick up the phone and have a real sales conversation with a prospect or a customer. You may recognise some of the symptoms below:

- Procrastinating instead of picking up the phone and dealing out. ie, scrolling through Facebook for the 15th time that hour.

- Getting involved with other activities and tasks that are not important at that time such as admin, filing or making yet another cup of coffee.

- Coming up with excuses on behalf of your clients before knowing the real answers. Such as; "They might be on their lunch," "I don't want to pester them," or "they would probably prefer I just email them."

- And finally, choosing to use 'easier' methods of contact such as text message or email despite not getting any responses over the past 20 emails you have sent.

I am sure there is an example above that resonates with you; either as something you have done yourself, or something you have recognised a team member doing. We have all gone through bouts of sales call reluctance and for some it could just depend on the mood we are in on a certain day.

There are whole books written just on the theories and psychology behind sales call reluctance and as much as I would love to talk to you about all of these now, I don't want to bore you. Of course, if you do want more information, or your whole team is struggling with sales call reluctance be sure to get in touch with us at Paragon Sales Solutions and we will gladly support you and train you. However in this chapter, I want to share with you my top four tips to help you overcome the fear of picking up the phone. If you ever feel yourself slipping into bad telesales habits, these tips will be sure to help you beat yourself out of the bad patch and get back on the phones.

Research

One of the reasons people may be wary to pick up the phone is down the feeling of being unprepared, and potentially worrying about feeling embarrassed if the call does not go well.

Before your next sales call, be sure to do a lot of research. Research everything you can about their business, what they may expect of you and also think about questions your prospect may ask. And of course, research the hell out of your own company and offering. The majority of the time, this kind of sales call reluctance stems from the fear of entering the unknown and to avoid making a fool out of ourselves or embarrassing ourselves. We can limit the chances of this happening by doing plenty of research on the prospect and our own products or services way before we pick up the phone.

Now here is the thing; don't waste too much time researching, otherwise you may find you spend time 'researching' to avoid making the call, which can lead to large periods of procrastination. Even just 10-15 minutes before your call can make all of the difference and with an abundance of knowledge available on the internet it should not take long at all - you could even start researching as you are waiting for the call to be put through or as the phone is dialling out. Do not mistake researching for procrastination.

Script

A lot of people are against sales scripts. No one wants a robot just reading a script line by line as this can come across fake and too rehearsed. However, having a simple guideline can work wonders; especially if you are going through a patch of low confidence. Once again, don't spend too long creating a sales script. My main advice here is to think about the line of questioning you need to uncover your prospect's pain points and your questions on how you will get to close the sale or to set up a follow up appointment.

The script itself can be written using the research you prepared earlier. A good script should be thought of as a road map. You can always use your social skills to enjoy a good sales conversation, but if you get lost or start to stumble, you have somewhere good to turn back to.

Don't be afraid to practice your script with a colleague or a superior either. As with anything in life, the more practice, the better!

Set Goals

Goals keep the world turning - we all know that. Without some form of goals and objectives we would just grind to a halt. And the same can be said for your telesales campaign.

By setting small, achievable goals you will not only fight to get the achievement of completing the goals, but you will turn it into a mini competition with yourself.

I would advise against targeting the amount of 'dials' or calls you make in a day. This rarely offers a true representation of what you need to achieve. Instead you want to be targeting the amount of contacts you have - as in, real conversations. Let's face it, dialling out and getting no answer will never get you a sale. But a real conversation, no matter how small, can lead to a sale.

Stand Up

I hark on about this a lot, but standing up when making sales calls can really improve your confidence and motivation. Tony Robbins, the great motivational speaker, says that 'motion is emotion' - and I have to side with him.

What happens when you are sat down all day? Or hunched over your desk? You become lethargic, right? Sitting down makes you feel weary, drained and ready for a nap.

But what happens when you stand up with your shoulders back? You feel powerful, you feel confident, and you feel energetic. Sometimes, when you are struggling to pick up that phone just the simple act of standing up can make you feel ten feet tall and re-energise you for a couple of hours of sales calls.

We all suffer from sales call reluctance from time to time and the issue truly comes into force when it becomes a habit. Sure, we all have a bad day from time to time but if that day becomes a couple of days, it could lead into a week, and so on. Use the above tips to stop yourself falling into a negative habit of failing to pick up the phone and see your sales naturally increase!

Handling Rejection

If you are new to sales, you need to get used to hearing the word 'no'.

If you are an experienced sales veteran you will probably be used to hearing that one, often painful, syllable.

Of course, reading this fantastic book (as well as my other books) will reduce your chances of being rejected whilst trying to sell, but the chances of being rejected are still very high. In fact, recent statistics show that for every minute of the day, sales people are rejected 1000 times around the globe (I did just make that statistic up, but if you know the true figures do be sure to email them over to me at; rob@paragonsalessolutions.co.uk)

Being rejected, and hearing the word no is very common when selling, and many will agree that the ability to pick yourself up and dust yourself down is what differentiates an average sales person to an elite salesperson. The greatest sales people in the world know how to take rejection, deal with it, and how to sometimes use that in their favour to eventually get the sale.

In this book we have already covered some objection handling and techniques and tactics that you can use to increase your chances of making the sale, but you know what? Sometimes things just don't work out. Sometimes you just don't get the sale - and that could be because you have lost out to a competitor or simply because your prospect has changed their mind completely and doesn't need what it is you are offering. Either way, we always have to remember that;

No doesn't mean no forever.

Repeat that again for me…

One of the biggest issues that any sales professional or business owner can create for themselves is that upon hearing the rejection, or whenever losing the sale, they can destroy the relationship that they have spent so long building, growing and developing. And this is very bad news indeed. If you destroy the business relationship for whatever reason, or throw your toys out of the pram, there is certainly no chance whatsoever you will ever get the sale in the future. Not only that, you will lose any chances of future recommendations or referrals. So if you get rejected, take the high ground, remain humble, and be there for your prospect when they may need you again.

This has happened to me first-hand.

At a networking event several years ago I met the owner of a Leicester based website. The website was focussed on local events within Leicester and was basically a 'what's on' guide for people in the area or people looking to visit. It did not take long for this guy to start talking to me about how great his website was, how many visitors it attracted per day, and how cost effective it was to advertise on the site. Sure, as I was looking at all of these numbers I did think it was a great marketing offer - however just not right for me or my business. It would have been fantastic for a Leicester based attraction, shop or restaurant or something, but for a sales consultant it would just be dead money. I told the chap that I would put some thought into it but at that time I didn't think it would be right, but encouraged him to reach out to me in the future all the same.

Several weeks later I received a message from him.

"Hi Rob, any news on the advertising banner on our website?"

"Hey," came my response, "yeah I have been thinking about it and I won't be going ahead. It just wouldn't be right for us. Thank you for the offer however."

The illusive 'dots' appeared on my screen as he was typing.

"Surprise surprise," he wrote back.

This response alone had me set back a bit. In my interpretation, it did seem bit blunt and a bit confrontational.

"Sorry to have kept you waiting on an answer," I typed back.

"What will be will be," they guy responded.

"I did see XYZ business recently and they told me that they are looking for new marketing opportunities. Is it worth me putting you in contact? Perhaps they may take you up on the offer."

"No, they aren't relevant, I am not interested. Thanks."

And that my friends, was that.

Despite me turning down an offer, which was a good offer I must say, and still trying to give a good referral this sales person ruined the relationship between me and him. It can of course be very damaging when you are rejected, on a personal level that is, but by throwing your toys out of the pram and sulking only makes things ten times worse. Had this chap remained humble and pleasant I am sure there could have been future business to be had there - but unfortunately due to a lack of long-term vision the business relationship dwindled and I have not seen or heard from this business or person in years.

There are some very important rules you should follow if you are constantly getting rejected:

Don't Take it Personally

The worst thing any sales professional can do is to take rejection personally.

If you hear a no, or you walk away from a meeting without a sale of course it can be very soul destroying, it can damage your confidence and it can leave you questioning yourself and your own ability.

Here's the secret though; when your prospect turns you down, they most likely are not rejecting you as a person!

Sure, there is a chance you may have upset or offended your prospect, but the chances of that should be very slim.

If you allow the rejection to plant a seed in your own esteem then it will only fester into further poor performance.

Remember; get yourself back up, dust yourself down, and get ready to go again.

Question the Objection

This is massive, and something we covered in the Objection chapter, but do not ever be afraid to question the objections or rejections. Confirm the reasons why you are being rejected. This will allow you the chance to maybe fix or solve any issues that your prospect is facing, i.e; the price is too high, or parts have not been explained fully yet etc.

Become a detective, find out the real reasons you are being turned away and either use them to your advantage and try to re-pitch or use the feedback for next customer.

Seek Feedback

If you are constantly being rejected and turned down, be sure to seek feedback from your colleagues, peers and even your superiors. Even your prospects and former customers if you have to.

Run through your sales pitch with those that are close to you and those that are willing to listen. Spend time with the best performing sales people in your office and try to learn all you can from them, and seek their advice and guidance. If need be, record your sales pitch on your phone and see where things are going wrong for yourself.

If you are willing to work on your sales pitches and proposals then eventually you will become the best sales person in your office.

Maintain the Relationship

The final note, is to keep the relationship open. Throwing your toys out of the pram, or avoiding your prospect and never talking to them again will just make you look like a muppet. So don't do it.

Keep in touch with them. Offer advice and value where

possible. Check in from time to time. Drop in some fruit or doughnuts to their office when you are passing by. Even if they have decided to go with a competitor; don't appear bitter.

Remember, a 'no' rarely means no forever. So keep in touch, keep the relationship open and you never know when that lost customer may become a paying customer down the line.

Public Speaking

There are times as a sales person or within your business where you will be asked to stand up and make a speech. It could be at a networking event, or could even be at your local school. Your local sports club perhaps? If this is the case, it is so important you are well prepared to get up and give a speech that even Churchill would be proud of.

You know what? My best advice for you is to get out there and give as many talks as you can. You see, when you give talks and presentations you slowly gain a reputation for becoming the expert in your chosen field. You become the 'go to' person for your industry and if this happens you can eventually get to a stage where people come to you asking for you products or service! Think of it this way; a health and safety consultant giving a speech on the importance of workplace safety, or how to reduce workplace absences to a room full of business owners will soon have people flocking to use you! Or imagine working for an accounts firm, giving a talk to a room full of entrepreneurs about the latest tax rules and regulations will lead people to remember you for the value you have delivered and will the audience turning to you for advice.

Speaking in public also gives you the chance to create incredible content that you can use again and again on your social media platforms. Think back to the chapter on Social Selling; the content you create can be shared on so many platforms if done correctly and can be used to gather new leads and solidify strong business relationships. The best thing you can do is to hire a professional photographer and/or videographer to document your speaking events. This might not be sustainable of course and for small speaking engagements at networking events it might seem a little overkill so if this is the case, arrive early and set up your phone (assuming you have a smartphone of course), put it on a tripod and set to record. From this phone footage alone you will have enough content to keep your YouTube, Twitter, Instagram and Facebook going for ages! And you can easily grab some stills from the footage if you wish.

Always record your speaking events in landscape (horizontal) and if you have anyone in the crowd taking photos, don't let them digitally zoom in; this way the content will be of a higher quality.

Public speaking, and presenting is something that some of us love to get up and do. However, for others, it can be a very nerve wrecking experience that can fill many full of dread and I intend this chapter to give you some fantastic tips to use moving forward.

No matter what your experience level is towards public speaking, it is important you get your presentation right – no one enjoys having to sit through a presentation that is below par.

In this quick chapter, allow me to share with you my top five most common presentation mistakes, and how by avoiding them, you can improve your presentation skills and become an incredible public speaker:

Under Preparation

Failing to prepare is preparing to fail – or so they say. Even the most dynamic, fun, and engaging speakers all prepare days and weeks in advance. Normally, public speaking nerves stem from the feeling of under preparation - similar to sales call reluctance.

So, before your next presentation take the time to practice your presentation. Practice the presentation in front of your friends, colleagues and loved ones. Ask them to provide feedback and ask for pointers. Record it yourself and watch it back if you have to. Make sure that the whole presentation flows, is full of value, and that you can reel it off at the drop of a hat.

The more work you do before the actual presentation or speech, the easier the talk will be when you finally get on stage. Sure, it will take extra time and you will still have to overcome some nerves when it comes to practising the speech in front of your colleagues, however it will be well worth it in the long run.

Not Engaging the Audience

Ask yourself this; are you presenting for you, or your audience?

Of course, the answer should be the audience. The reason you are speaking at an event is for your audience and so it is safe to say you should engage them as best you can, and to lay down the foundations as to what they can expect from the talk.

We have all been in a talk or presentation when we have no idea when it is due to end, or what will be involved – and this can lead us to feel restless. So help your audience out and let them know what to expect, and when!

You can do this by laying out an agenda or simply explaining clearly what you are going to talk about.

There is a chapter later on in this book that focusses more on how to captivate an audience so for more support and tips on how to keep an audience listening to you then be sure to give that a read!

Over Indulging a Visual

Does the term 'death by PowerPoint' ring a bell to you? What happens when you stick on a PowerPoint slide that is FULL of content? Your audience stop listening to YOU, and they read the SLIDE.

I believe that a good slide should just be a tease. Or a little hint of what you are talking about. A small suggestion as to what you are talking about. This way, you are giving away some content for your audience to read and digest but you are not taking the spotlight away from you.

So, on your slides, stick to bullet points, headlines and photos if possible. Your audience are there to listen to you speak – so let them!

You could even break up your presentation with a video if you so wish. A video in the middle of a presentation gives you the perfect chance to take a breath, sip some water, and get ready for the next part of your talk.

Avoiding Eye Contact

It does not matter the size of the crowd; the better a personal connection you can make with your audience the better. You will be remembered easier, and your audience will go away full of praise for you.

Keep your notes to a minimum, and avoid staring at the walls, the floor, the ceiling and the presentation. The more eye contact, the better.

This is why having shorter slides works so well. If your audience are just gawping at a presentation, they most certainly are not looking at your beautiful face. And if you are not giving your audience eye contact they are only going to be thinking about what they are having for dinner or planning out some emails they need to send when they get back to the office.

Not Preparing for the Venue

How embarrassing is it when you sit down, ready to take in a great talk and the speaker can't get the projector to work. Next thing you know the clicker stops working. And then, the microphone drops out so the people in the back can't hear. And then all the lights turn off. Or there is a large pillar in the way stopping half of the audience from taking in the talk and staying focussed.

It does not matter how good your public speaking is, and how professionally put together your presentation is; it is these small factors that your audience will remember the most. So as part of your preparation, arrive to the venue early, familiarise yourself with the space and the equipment and if you get the chance, do a practice run in the same space with the same equipment as you will on the big day! It does not matter if you are speaking at a networking group of 10 people, or a conference with 2000 people; prepare, prepare, prepare!

Everyone's a Customer

I think to get my point across in this chapter I need to start with a story.

Most people know that during my employed life as a sales manager of a fine food supplier, I used to cycle to and from the office. I did it for years and was one of the greatest decisions I have ever made. Don't get me wrong, it did have it's negatives; the wind and rain weren't ideal, and my ass didn't look the best in Lycra (and I did get knocked off my bike on several occasions), but the health benefits far outweighed the negatives and not only that, it shaved off around 25 minutes commuting time every day and saved me a fair penny or two too!

To help shave off some time on my commute, before I reached my office I used to cut through a large car dealership's forecourt. It probably only saved me a minute or two to do so, but it all adds up doesn't it. This one particular day, I was feeling more tired than normal and decided to get off my bike and walk through the forecourt instead of cycling. This gave me the opportunity to see 3 of the forecourts sales people as they were heading for their morning cigarette.

As I approached the three men, all smartly dressed and enjoying their first coffees of the day, I made sure to look up and try to make eye contact. And I did; I looked up, clocked eyes with one of the sales people and slightly nodded my head and said 'morning' – believe it or not, I got blanked. Yes, that is right. I got completely blanked by this sales person. He quickly looked away and continued to talk to his colleagues about the crap he got up to at the weekend.

Now, I am not one to assume, however it got me wondering why I was blanked. I thought it over; my approach was friendly enough, and not overly friendly either. The only thing I could put it down to was two things;

Perhaps the exchange was too early for this individual. Maybe he hadn't quite woken up at this time of the morning. Or, on the assumption of what I was wearing (cheap cycling gear), the individual assumed I could not afford one of his fine cars.

Unfortunately, both of these reasons don't sit well with me at all. First of all, it is never too early to sell. As soon as your eyes open you should be ready and raring to go.

As a sales person you must be ready to sell at any given opportunity. I don't care if you are too tired, or if you are hungover or whatever. They are all of YOUR problems. Not your customers!

Secondly, the assumption that I could not afford a shiny new car is a terrible excuse to not approach me! My current car was falling apart, and I was starting to think about getting a new car. Just because I didn't walk across the forecourt in smart shoes and wearing my suit didn't mean I couldn't afford a car; it just means I prefer to wear Lycra (true story).

Back in May of 2017 I read a story which underlines this point completely. An elderly man walked into a shop called Maxsingburibigbike in Thailand. This man was dressed in clothes that were very aged and just wearing old flip flops. As the man looked around the shop, sales people ignored him thinking he was just looking around and wasting time. Because he didn't look like he had money, he was ignored. Despite giving off plenty of buying signals and focusing his attention to a bike that cost just over $17,000 still no one approached him, so he went off to find the store owner. After a 10-minute chat with the owner, the gentleman proceeded to pay for the bike in cold hard cash.

You should never judge a book by it's cover!

The point I am getting at is that every person you come in to contact with as a sales person or a business is a customer; either current, or future. They also know people that could potentially become your customers too if you treat them well and with respect.

I tell my teams, and people I coach, to never judge anyone on what they want or do not want. Never assume what your customer wants. A good sales person will speak with a prospect and ask them what THEY want. It is then your job to problem solve and recommend the right product or service to satisfy the needs of your prospect. The minute you withhold a product or service just under the assumption your client doesn't want it or cannot afford it is the day you need to address your mindset and question whether or not you truly want to sell.

On a side note to this – just because a prospect is not your customer NOW doesn't't mean that they won't be your customer in the future! Treat every person you meet with the utmost respect and do not feel ill feelings towards a prospect if after you have spent time with them that they go away and think things over. For all you know, your prospect will return in a month's time, two months' time, maybe even a years' time! Business at times can be a slow-moving wheel and you have to be ready to take any chance you are given.

So, thinking back to my earlier story – the scenario where I was ignored by 3 sales people. Just imagine if they had opened me up and got to know me a little bit, even day by day. If, from that first initial contact these people had tried to develop a relationship with me I would be more than willing to buy from them. This could be worth £15,000 or so to their company, and God knows how much it is worth to this person's pay slip! But as it stands, my mind is still open to options across the market and only time will tell where I eventually decide to buy a new car from.

This happens all too often; we make excuses in our own heads as to why a customer may not buy. But all this does is limit your chances of ever making a sale as you will be put off from ever asking a prospect and engaging them in a conversation. You should never, ever assume what a prospect may want, or can afford. Ultimately, let the customer decide. And always give the customer the chance to tell you what he or she would like.

Remember; it is all about questioning!

Unbeatable Telesales

Selling over the phone for many can be a very daunting and petrifying task. Even just having a conversation on the phone can send shivers of dread through many. Believe me, I have been there. And so too have thousands and thousands of people all of whom have felt that small tremble before dialling out over the telephone.

It is nothing to be ashamed of. The art of selling over the phone is near enough vital to making your business succeed, or to help your business to grow. Sure, at Paragon we are proud ambassadors of modern techniques in selling such as social selling, and even traditional methods such as face to face selling. However, at times nothing beats a good old fashioned telephone call. If you truly want to get the sale, and to boost your profits you need to pick up the phone, and have a conversation with the person on the other end of it.

Although slightly dated now, I found some statistics to back up my feelings towards the importance to telesales and telemarketing. According to Hubspot, 68% of B2B sales involved some form of human interaction. This includes contact from Telemarketing and telesales. They went on to say also:

It takes 80 calls on average to get an opportunity.

In a poll of business managers, B2B telesales calls at work were voted as the least annoying form of advertising. Only 4% said it was the most annoying form, while the eight other options were all voted more annoying.

Almost 60% of marketing managers in fortune 500 companies say telemarketing is "Very Effective" for leads and customer outreach, and when those who say it is only "Effective" that percentage is almost over 90%.

Short campaigns for direct marketing do not work, on average it takes no less than 3 months for a company to start seeing real results.

70% of business to business sales comes from human interaction which 56% of which started with telemarketing.

Sure, these statistics are from 2015, so could be slightly out, but they do make for interesting reading. So whether you are a small company looking to boost brand awareness, or a medium sized company looking to set up more meetings for your sales reps - at times nothing beats picking up the phone!

And by telesales, I need to point out I am not talking about row upon row of people picking up the phone, reading from a script daring to stray too far away from the written words in front of them. The best form of telesales is exactly what I mentioned before: a conversation. It is a good old fashioned 'chin wag' but with direction. A fact finding conversation, a value giving conversation, and a way to develop a business relationship far better than a Facebook or LinkedIn post ever could.

At Paragon, we run telemarketing campaigns for companies up and down the UK. Although we do pride ourselves on our sales rates and our ability to close sales, the one thing I always look for from the team is relationship development. We believe strongly in the need to get to know our prospects and our potential customers so that we can understand their needs and work alongside them to find the best solution to their problem.

And you should do too.

Sure; if you have the budget (and it could be cheaper than you think!) you should leave the telephone calls to the professionals. The Paragon team have been doing this for years and are well equipped to get the sale on your behalf. But if you want a more hands on approach to your sales process, then I am happy to share our top tips for telesales success.

All of these tips are best prescribed with practice. The more you work on your skills, just like anything in life, you will become an expert in no time at all. But in the meantime, enjoy these tips. Learn from them. Put them into practice. And be sure to let me know how you get on!

Smile Down The Telephone

This may sound a little odd, but it works. The person on the other phone will pick up on it. I assure you. It is funny how we can pick up the emotions of others and how that rubs off on us. The cheerier you are, the happier your prospect will be. The happier your prospect, the more likely they will be to buy from you.

Check Your Attitude

With every new call comes a fresh chance. Don't let your mood affect your next call. It doesn't matter if you have just had the phone put down on you 20 times in a row, or if you have closed the biggest sale of your life on the previous call; start every dial afresh and hit the reset button every time you pick up the phone.

Stand Up

An improved posture will improve your speech, reaction time and ability to think on your feet (literally).

Standing up also allows you to feel much more energised. As we discussed earlier in the chapter about sales call reluctance; if you are slouched down in a negative position over your desk this is going to affect how you sound over the phone.

Stand up, shoulders back and feel proud!

Be Prepared

Taking the time to research your prospect, their company and understand all of the inner details of your own product or service will help during any conversation. You don't want to be 'Umm' - ing or 'Err' - ing too much! The more of an expert you sound the better. This will allow you to control the conversation much better and will give you plenty of confidence when it comes to handling the flow of the conversation.

Question

Questions are more important than statements. Asking your prospect the right questions will you keep you on track to get the sale.

Remember; a phone call is no different really to a conversation that would occur face to face. Use your normal approach to a physical conversation and you will be just fine.

Keep Going

If you have a successful call, do not stop to celebrate. Keep going and celebrate later! Sometimes being on a roll will help your campaign. It can be tempting to run off to make a cup of tea, to smoke a cigarette, or to celebrate with your peers. Whilst you are feeling good and in form; keep going!

Count the Contact - Not The Calls

Let's say you have a list of 20 people to call in one day. Don't keep a tally after every call you make. Count every CONTACT you have had. Just because the person on your list did not pick up their phone does not mean you can tick them off your list.

At Paragon, we do not set targets on the amount of dials made. I would much prefer the team to have 5 successful or promising conversations in an hour than just dialling 25 times in an hour. Dials do not equal success.

Make One More Call

Before you stop for a tea break. Or before you stop for lunch. Before you stop for the day, make one more call. The top earners and top performers always go that extra mile.

Just one more call could mean the difference between success and failure.

Sound Interested

Whilst on the phone and having conversations, don't just go through the motions. Don't ask your prospect questions and then glaze over whilst checking your Instagram feed. Use active listening. Truly care for what the other person on the other end of the phone is telling you. Be sure to repeat back to them the key points and prove to them that you are listening. Not only will this develop a strong business relationship but will ensure that you are ensuring the points they are telling you and will give you a better chance of selling to them down the line.

Make Friends

Be sure to be nice, friendly and polite to people. Even if they do not want your offer; treat everyone with respect. Make sure you are remembered for the right reasons! We always buy from people we like, and as I have mentioned in this book 100 times already, by building strong relationships you will see a greater chance of success whether it be immediately or even years down the line.

What to do When Sales are Down

It happens from time to time; sales drop. Sales people are not performing to their usual high standard, figures are dropping, and no matter what anyone tries everything just seems to fail and die a death.

When sales start to dry up, it can be a very demoralising time, a worrying time in fact. As a business, sales are of course very important. Do you even have a business if you are not selling?

There are many reasons why sales might start to drop off and the reasoning behind it could be long-winded and might take weeks or even months to get back on track using a solid sales and marketing plan. However the key thing to remember is to not panic. Panicking and panic selling will only cause problems down the line. Another thing to do is to recognise when things start to go wrong early. The earlier you recognise sales are dropping, or individuals within the business are not performing the sooner you can put a plan into action, help and mentor those around you and you can ultimately get the sales pointing in the direction they should; and that is up!

Although this whole chapter could perhaps be written on a business level and we could look at sales on a business scale, I want to tailor this for you; the individual. Whether you are an entrepreneur, business owner or even a sales professional, this chapter will give you the hints, tips and support to see a quick turn around in your own sales process.

If you are suffering a drop in sales as a business be sure to contact the Paragon Sales Solutions team and we can step in to take a look at your whole sales and marketing plan and see how we can help; the last thing I ever want to see is a business die out due to a lack of sales!

Let's get one thing straight; even the best sales people go through highs and lows in form. You cannot expect a top sales person to be at the top of their game consistently. Sure; it would be nice if they were! But sales people are human beings like the rest of us with their own personal lives and other factors going on in their lives.

As a sales professional at heart, I have been there myself. I have seen my sales go through the roof and I have been able to smash every target ever handed to me. But there has also been times when I couldn't sell for the life of me and I seemed to see my form drop off. I liken it to when a footballer's confidence goes down; a striker whom normally is collecting 20 goals a season starts to struggle to get anywhere near the target. The talent is still there, but the confidence and the form is not.

So what can you do when you see your sales start to go down? Here are my top three tips to overcome a sales slump on an individual level:

Slow Down

Whenever we see a sales slump, or see our sales fall it can be very natural to run around like a busy fool and to panic. We can start to panic sell; selling everything at a discount. We could start calling up old customers and prospects we haven't spoken to in 5 years expecting the business relationship to still be intact and begging them to buy from us again. This can do more harm than good at times - and the last thing you should do is panic.

The key thing you need to do? Slow down!

If you panic, and rush around, it can be very easy to put pressure on prospects which is only going to push the buyer away. Rushing only leads to wrong decisions being made. This can later lead to buyers remorse and people falling out with you. Believe it or not, us consumers can smell a mile off when a sales person is behind on their targets!

An hour or two assessing and gathering feedback on your performance can make all the difference!

Take a step back. Assess what is going wrong. Are you targeting the wrong audience? Have you made misjudgments in your pricing structure? Are you pitching your product or service in the wrong way?

Slow down, regroup, and look to build on that.

Switch to a More Consultative Approach

The consultative selling approach is where a sales person becomes more of a consultant for their prospect, and the sales person will act as a guide and help the prospect find the right solution for their problem.
Think back to what you read in the very first chapter of this book and imagine yourself as a doctor. All a doctor does is ask their patient questions, and from these answers the doctor can then prescribe the best solution and medication. You can easily do the same once you are in front of your prospect and potential customers.

If we think back to step one for a second – sales could be down because you are trying to sell what YOU want to sell for YOUR reasons, and not selling for the BUYERS reasons.

A consultative approach will allow you as a sales person to slow things down, to listen to the buyer and to adapt your sales approach for their needs.

It is amazing what happens when we ask our customers and prospects what they want!

Stay Positive

We all know that a positive mindset can help us achieve anything. And as cheesy as it sounds – it's true.

Let's look back to the analogy of the footballer for a minute; the striker whom was once a 20 goal a year hitman is now struggling to get a shot on target. What happens if the striker allows his head to drop? What happens when they start to doubt their ability? Confidence drops lower and it becomes a very dark cycle of underperformance mixed with low self-esteem and low confidence.

When your sales start to drop; stay positive. Lift your head up. Keep smiling. You will achieve a sale again – you just need to put the above to points into your daily sales activities and you will see a massive change in your fortunes.

I know that can be hard. When sales are down you can start to question yourself, your ability and your career choices. But ultimately as long as you are selling a good product or service, and you have every confidence in the pricing structure and can recognise the benefits your product or service can bring to your customers then you will be foolish to quit now!

One thing I used to do when my sales were down was to talk to my customers. I used to seek feedback about the product, the service and ultimately the customer experience; including their experience of me. It is from this reflection and feedback I was able to pick myself up and push forward.

Sure, everyone is different and you will pick yourself up in different ways to me. You might find watching an inspirational movie will fire you up, or even a motivational podcast. Whatever you need to do; just do it! You will thank yourself later once you see your sales figures working better in your favour and the targets being met once again.

Don't Discount; Add Value

I hate discounts.

Whoa, wait a moment. OK - Let me reword that. I don't want to lie to you. I love receiving discounts. Who doesn't?! We all love having 10% off an item or even 50% off. Bargains turn us on!

We all love a sale and there is no hiding from the fact even the word SALE can drive us crazy and turn our healthy bank balances into crumbling numbers with overdrafts looming.

What I meant to say, is that I hate GIVING discounts. That doesn't mean I am tight, stingy and am money obsessed. However discounting an item or even a service makes me wince in pain and agony.

Discounting an item is too easy of an opening statement and simply means something in the marketing strategy of a product or a service has gone wrong. There are companies out there who simply rely on discount strategies (you all have seen that one shop that is always 'closing down'!) and this is just an endless cycle of failure.

To me, discounting an item to get the sale proves the following things;

1. The seller has no confidence in the product.
2. The seller has no confidence in themselves.
3. The seller has not marketed the product well enough.
4. The seller has made a mistake.

Please do not get me wrong; there are times when a product simply needs to be discounted as it is simply dead weight in an inventory or the line needs to be gone to make way for a new wave of product. In these terms, yes ok I agree with you a discount is needed and is possibly the easiest way to turnover a product in a short amount of time.

Discounting an item straight away or even offering money off a service straight away is not a good touch. You may feel like that you are making the price look sexy, or you might feel you are doing your customer a favour, or you want to make the item seem like a bargain for a quick sale - but are you just underselling yourself?

My argument is this; if you are willing to discount something so early on within the sales process or straight off the bat, are you even confident in what it is you are selling? Better still; are you confident in your own sales skills? What I constantly coach my team and what I ask them to do is to always be strong in their approach to negotiations and to understand the importance of what it is they are selling. If a certain product can be sold at a cheaper price; why isn't it just set at that cheaper price? A price is set for a very valid reason.

This used to happen to me a lot when I used to buy and sell antiques and pieces of art. The amount of times I would hear, "What is your best price?" Or "How low will you go on this?" - I think Bargain Hunt has a lot to answer for here. But anyway, my response was always that the price was firm - if I could offer it cheaper I would just list the price at that cheaper price!

People always want things cheaper and at a discount and one way to better yourself when it comes to fighting off discounts is to **ADD VALUE**.

Adding value should be included in the initial package of the product or service in my opinion. Adding little extras to the deal or even adding your expertise and your knowledge can make or break a deal at times but why again should you hold these back from your customer straight away? Once again, it is just another dishonest action to take and all cards should be placed on the table from the start in my opinion.

Adding value is nothing new, however as mentioned above can make your product or service stand out from a field of haggled prices and discounted options. Adding value is your choice, and whatever you add to your deal must be relevant and of course be tempting to the buyer. Added value can even simply be a guarantee, or warranty of work, or even if you have built a solid reputation for fairness and good quality workmanship the added value could be the fact they are buying from you; a reputable sales person.

Even recently, we were searching for a better broadband and telephone package for Paragon Sales Solutions. Of course, so many companies were trying to beat each other on price and were trying to undercut each other. In the end, I went with the service that I felt I would get the best service from. And I am not talking about service as in broadband strength or download and upload speeds. I mean the service I would get from a company; in this scenario, this was the added value. It was made clear that I would have one main point of contact that I could call upon for any help and support and this person would help the business to grow by offering their expertise. It was this added value that stopped me going for a cheaper option!

So next time a customer is asking for a discount, don't forget to slow things down. Instead of thinking about what you can take away from the deal, think about what you can ADD to the deal - and I am confident you will see your sales go up and up.

But having said all of that, what happens if you do all of the above, provide more value and yet your prospect still asks for a discount? Here are my three top tips to overcoming the price objection and to stop giving away your precious profit margins:

Clarify the objection

People will tend to use the price objection as a way to hide behind the fact they do not want to buy your product or service, or do not trust you. So, first of all, why not ensure that it is actually the price of the product or service that is putting them off and not the whole idea of your product or service and offering.

The simple question of; "If this was completely free of charge, is this the product/service you would opt for?" Of course, if they say yes then you know for sure that they have a need in what it is you are selling so you can look to address the pricing issue in a way that suits you and the customer.

Sell the value

Normally discounting a product or service too soon can undervalue the offering far too quickly. I don't know about you, but it really turns me off when people can create a 50% discount out of thin air; it leaves a bitter taste in my mouth. I understand every business needs to make profit, however sometimes it can be sickening when you learn just how steep some profit margins can be.

Here, you can either add value on to your sale to try to make the deal sound more appealing; such as adding £100 of services to your package as opposed to discounting by £100. Or, you can discuss the return of investment that your offering will provide, or the long term savings that your offering will deliver. If your offering will save your prospect £20 in labour per day then remind them. If your offering will be able to provide a return of investment then be sure to remind your prospect of those facts!

Stay quiet

Sometimes, a bit of silence speaks louder than words. If you are ever faced with an objection, not necessarily just a price objection, a bit of silence will encourage the prospect to speak up and to explain their reasoning. It is from this explanation that you can then try to find the right solution that will not only suit your prospect, but your business too.

Remember; if a prospect is asking for a discount it does normally mean that they are interested in your product or service. I always say that a prospect asking for a discount is perhaps one of the biggest and strongest buying signals you could ever expect to hear.

But be warned; do not be so quick to discount your offering. Hold your ground, sell the value and allow the prospect to explain their reasoning!

Making the Most of Networking

Business networking events are a fantastic way to make new connections, interact with other business owners and to also look for new avenues of business. Networking has been a solid staple of business owners and sales professionals alike for decades and that simply proves that it does work, if done in the right way of course.

This is one of the many reasons why I decided to set up the Leicestershire Business Network Group.

It is clear to see and understand that if you truly want to fill your sales pipeline full of great opportunities and if you want to ensure you have solid relationships with other people then networking is the way to do it. But for me, I found other networking groups too expensive, too rule obsessed, and too 'clicky'. I wanted to create amazing networking opportunities for businesses of any size without the need to take out a business loan to join, and where people would enjoy going; even if they don't want to talk about business. One thing is for sure; so much business is passed around at these events it is unreal. When you allow people to talk and converse in a natural and unforced manner magical things can happen, but only if you use your time networking effectively.

If you have yet to get out and network then I strongly do urge you to give it a go. There are plenty of networking events out there and although some might not suit you and the way you work, there will be plenty that do. A simple search online will give you access to hundreds of networking events close by to you, at differing times of the day and at different budgets.

If you do decide to start networking, my key piece of advice to you is to be consistent with it. You cannot go to just one networking meeting or event and expect to come away with lots of sales or plenty of opportunities. Just like any other kind of relationship; things take time. People want to get to know you and people want to learn about you and develop that all important trust. And the only way to do this is to remain consistent, to keep showing your face and to keep having conversations with people.

A networking event is simply a chance to plant seeds; but if you do not water or tend to those

seeds then nothing will grow.

In my eyes, there are three crucial reasons why you should consider networking. These reasons are leads, research and development, and connections. You and I both know that the number one reason you should network is to gather leads and to generate interest in your business. I will share some ideas shortly how you can use these leads to your advantage and how to make the most of them.

Networking events also give you the chance to stay up to date with the latest news and advice for businesses and you may get to learn some fantastic things from speakers and other presentations. Working in sales, and owning a business can at times become frustratingly lonely and isolating and if you can find networking events near you that offer some form of educational or motivational talk then you should be sure to attend as the knowledge you pick up could help you to drive your business and your sales forward.

The connections made at networking events are the most valuable entity in my eyes. Sure, some of these connections may not become direct customers themselves however you will be given the chance to come face to face and to converse with influential people that could either pass referrals your way or might even be willing to offer you support, guidance and support when you require it.

It is crucially important that business networking is taken seriously, and you use your time to your advantage. I still experience, and witness so many people networking in the wrong ways. Perhaps 'wrong' is not the right word to use here, because I guess there is no wrong or right way to business network. However, there are so many people I see and talk to whom network ineffectively. Your time is money. And if you are not looking for sales or business opportunities and only attending networking events to drink with your old chums or people you already know then you are only wasting your time.

If you want to network effectively, and see the greatest results from your time, here are my three top tips to help you make the most out of networking:

Work the Room

At any business event, you have the chance to mingle and chat with business owners of many shapes and sizes. You also get the chance to start conversations with people that could prove beneficial to your business; either as a new supplier, or as a new client or customer. With this in mind, don't get stuck talking to people that you know very well, and you are familiar with.

This happens all too often. You see someone in the crowd that you know and whilst feeling either anxious or nervous to approach new people you go over and strike conversation. You end up reminiscing about the past or start to chat about the last time you played golf together. Before you know it, other business owners in the room start to filter away and the networking event is over. You have missed your chance to set up those all important new connections.

So, do your very best to mix and mingle with people you have never laid eyes on before. Sure, do go and speak to the people you already know as this will further develop business relationships. But don't forget to break away and mingle with new connections.

You could even try setting yourself a target on the amount of conversations you have at an event, or the amount of business cards you can collect.

Be social. Work the room. Converse with others!

Offer Value

Believe me; there is nothing more boring than entering a conversation with someone and being spoken to for 15 minutes about their business without having a chance to get a word in edge ways. When this happen our eyes glaze over and we start to think of other things.

It can be very tempting when we meet new business people to waffle on about what we do, how amazing we are, and why we are so great. Trust me, the person you have just met does not really care too much about all of that.

Instead, be a person of value. Ask questions. See how you can help or support that business owner. Is there anyone you can introduce the other to? Do you have a connection that can support the person in front of you? Can you help them fix the issue they have been having with their bookkeeping system? Or perhaps, by asking meaningful questions, you can distinguish pain points that your business offerings can help to solve?

Always listen more than you talk! You will always open up more doors this way that will allow you to walk into.

But don't forget to be willing to run through your elevator pitch and look to connect with the person you are talking to. It is all about balance.

Always Follow Up

After every networking event, be sure to send introductory emails to everyone you spoke with. Using the business cards you have collected, send a simple introductory email that helps to develop the business relationship further.

It does not have to be a long email; a simple few lines thanking them for their time, how you enjoyed the conversation and how you look forward to chatting with them sooner can suffice.

Do not copy and paste a general message either. And don't just send out a blanket email and blind copy everyone in Make the emails personal. Mention things you both spoke about. Show the connection that you care!

But, a word of warning! Do not start trying to pitch or sell anything to your connection in the first email. It can be really off putting! Sure, if your connection has shown a strong interest in what you offer then email them and look to set up a secondary meeting or if they have requested it, send over some information and prices etc. But, do not send an email pitching what you offer in this first email. You will only push your new connection away and may damage the relationship in the long term.

Keep it friendly. Keep it open. And keep it personal!

Using Your Voice

Sales can be made or lost simply down to the way we communicate. Of course, a successful sales person should know that it is far more important to listen than it is to speak, however the ability to talk is vitally important during a sales conversation – understandably.

We already discussed earlier on in the book how Professor Albery Mehrabian published his studies in the 1970's that suggested that we deduce our feelings, attitudes and beliefs about what someone says not by the actual words spoken, but by the speaker's body language and tone of voice - with tone of voice making up 55% of the importance in how we communicate. This is why the voice is so important, not just for telesales or conversations on the phone but also in face to face sales opportunities too.

The way in which we speak and how we set our voice can help to make or break a sale and is also something that so few of us put into good practice. I have worked with sales coaching clients whom have a much greater intelligence than I, understand the sales cycle very well and have a strong passion for sales and yet struggle to sell; and sometimes this is down to their voice and how they use it.
Don't worry; I am not going to expect you to conduct any chants during this chapter. Nor am I going to send you on a singing lesson course. This chapter has been written to help you to pay attention to your voice and to understand how it can affect your sales. And once we master our voice and understand it more it can become another tool to our sales kit that will help us see an increase in our sales.

Here are five simple tips that will help you to take control of your voice and will allow you to understand in great depth how your voice can play a part in how you sell.

Take Your Prospect on a Journey

There are few things less exciting than going on a fast car ride, a fast rollercoaster or listening to fast tempo music. The same can be said for your voice. The faster the tempo of your voice the more you will get your prospect excited and they will want to join you on that conversational journey. Increase the speed of your voice and the words you are using to build up your conversational excitement and use this to build up the desire in what you are saying.

Put the Brakes on

Asking for the sale is the most important part of a sales conversation. Sure, you can sell and describe all of the benefits and go through the pricing plan with your prospect and yet if you do not ultimately ask for the sale at the end of your pitch then you will rarely, or never, make a sale.

Some people get nervous at this stage of the sales process and tend to speed up. Many get so anxious they try to rush past this crucial stage of the sales process, but this once again just masks the key points and questions along in all of the excitement that you have already built, and you can skip over the minor details. At this stage of the sales conversation you should try to slow down your speech on the words that need emphasising which will help to highlight the point you are trying to make.

The change in tempo will also ensure that the prospects attention is regained, and they too can start to allow decisions to be made. Everyone notices a quick change in pace. When you learn how to control them tempo of your voice you will soon be able to control many a conversation.

Watch the Volume

No one likes being spoken to. And no one likes people raising their voice at them.

Sure, a loud statement can help to grab someone's attention and to emphasise points but sometimes this can be too harsh for the smaller details to be heard.

Instead of raising your voice, why not try whispering?

A great trick is to lower your voice at the key aspects and near enough whisper certain parts of your sales pitch that you believe should be highlighted. When we whisper we do two things; we attract the prospect closer to us and encourage them to lean forward so that they have to listen harder both physically and mentally. The prospect will listen harder to ensure they understand what you are saying. Also, you will give the impression that you are telling them a secret, something that no one else should know. This will help to develop a strong rapport with your prospect and will also suck them in for the most important parts of your pitch.

Stop Talking

As we mentioned earlier, when asking for the sale many of us can get over excited and can actually talk ourselves out of the sale. Have you ever pitched your product or service to someone, asked for the sale, and then felt the need to try to justify the pricing, or try to go over again why the prospect should buy from you? This is a big 'no no' in sales. When you do this, you over take your prospects thought process. You stop them from making the decision and enter into a new conversation, and then you then have to re-ask for the sale! So you have done a full circle.

Next time you ask for the sale, or finalise your pitch, just stay quiet. It can be very hard to do, and may feel a little awkward at first, but you will see your sales increase dramatically. So, what you expect to hear is:

"So, Mrs. Prospect, if we get you signed up now that will cost you £140."

Stay quiet.

Wait for your prospect to speak. This returns the power to the prospect to say yes and will give them a chance to ask further questions or offer objections if needed.

Breathe Goddammit, Breathe!

Our voices are powerful tools. And yet the engine that truly powers our voice is our breath. Breathing correctly will give us the chance to put the above voice tools to good use, will reduce stress and will allow us to remain in complete control of the sales conversation.

Remember; your brain won't function without oxygen. So if you are not providing it with some beautiful air then you will not be able to think on your feet and operate at a high standard.

Take the time to breathe and use simple pauses and gaps in your pitch to breathe which in turn will help to empathise the key points in your pitch that you are trying to get across.

The Bigger Picture

Sometimes, we all have to take a step back, take a breath, and think things over.

It can be very frustrating when you perfectly pitch your product or service to someone whom you have qualified professionally, and despite your best efforts to follow up with them, they do not come back to you. Or they ignore you. Or they keep palming you off and you eventually lose the sale.

If this happens, do not take things personally. And do not lose your patience with your prospect. You see, your product or your service might not be your prospect's biggest concern right now. Your prospect has their own life. Their own job. Their own family. Life can get in the way at times and can distract even the most hardworking of us. So don't take it personally and react badly if someone you are trying to sell to is dawdling or not responding to you.

When we own our own business, or spend our days talking about and pitching a certain product, it of course becomes one of the most important aspects of our lives. It is all we think about, all we care about and all we want to talk about. We wake up thinking about it, we go to sleep thinking about it; ultimately what we sell becomes our life.

But, just because it is *your* main concern and *your* main priority does not mean it is your prospects main concern or number one priority.

Later on this book I am going to share with you why it is important to follow up with prospects, and why you should continue to follow up with potential customers until you hear a definitive no. And this chapter serves as a gentle reminder to keep your emotions in check whilst doing so. and to not feel negative, or make your prospect feel bad if they are too busy for you.

You see, unless your product or service is absolutely the matter of life and death for your prospect, or they are utterly desperate for it, then you will never be their number one priority. They have a million and one other things to care about and worry about; their business life, personal life, and even social life. All of these things take a greater priority than your sales pitch.

This will happen within your sales career: you have a prospect that is just dragging their heels, it is very important that you do what I wrote about in the opening sequence of this chapter; take a step back, take a breath, and think things over. Don't rush anything, and do not apply too much pressure. Many sales trainers and sales coaches preach to people that they must force their offerings down their prospects neck and to not allow them time to think – and although this can work to a degree, it can also lead to a higher level of buyer's remorse and dissatisfaction down the line and will ultimately push your prospect away. Surely if you are having to force a buyer into buying your product or service then you haven't sold the benefits effectively and the value that you can bring to them.

In my eyes, you should be giving your prospect more time to think things over and give them the patience that they so deserve. Give your potential customer the power. If you appear desperate to push the sale over the line is that going to give your prospect the confidence that what you have to sell is worth the wait?

So next time you are waiting to hear back from a prospect just remember this; we all have a million and one other things going on in our lives right now and your sales pitch is just a small building block of that.

So be kind, be patient and be empathetic. Sure, do follow up with your prospect as we will come on to later on in this book as it will at the least remind them that you are there for them and will help to keep you at the forefront of their mind. But do not fall out with them or throw your toys out of the pram because they have taken more than a day to respond to your email. As I keep saying; business relationship development is the most crucial skill to a successful sales career so always remain empathetic and await success.

Remember; take a breath, be patient, and be there when your prospect does need you.

Consultative Selling

Consultative selling is a phrase that has been around for a while and is used by many sales professionals still do this day. And in fact, I have already used it in this book several times.

In this chapter, I want to share with you the meaning of consultative selling, why you should use this good practice and how, in doing so, you will see a massive increase in your sales.

Over most recent years, the increase of key terms in sales such as 'social selling' has seen 'consultative selling' to fall down in the pecking order of sales techniques and terms and yet should still be considered as one of the biggest and most effective sales tactics available. And some may argue that consultative selling is the foundation of social selling anyhow.

In a nut-shell, consultative selling is the act in which a sales person plays the role of a consultant. The sales person will assist the buyer and to help them to identify their needs and will then act to satisfy those needs where possible. It is really as simple as that. Some of the biggest examples of stereotypical consultative sales people are those that sell custom software packages, or communication specialists. These guys and girls will sit down with a business and understand their pain points and then prescribe the right solution to fix those issues.

Consultative selling is the back bone that all sales people should be using in their sales process no matter how long that sales cycle is. Historically consultative selling has been reserved for longer sales processes and larger purchases in which the sales person can have more patience and develop a stronger rapport with their prospect. However, I am a firm believer that consultative selling can also be very beneficial for smaller sales cycles including retail sales. I used to take the very same approach when I used to sell for a large DIY based retail store. I used to sit back, and listen to whatever it was a customer would tell me and ultimately prescribe the best product possible; even it it was something we could not offer.

You see, no consumer ever wants to feel like just another sales target. No consumer wants to feel like a number. They want to feel like they well looked after, appreciated and that they have also received the best possible product or service for their investment. You yourself are a consumer too, and you are a buyer. How do you want a sales person to treat you?

Ultimately, consultative selling allows you the chance to be more patient, to allow for a stronger business relationship with your prospect to be formed and for you to truly understand the needs and requirements that your prospect wants you to meet. Think back to the very first chapter of this book in which we discussed questioning, and how if you ask more questions and just become a problem solver then you will naturally see an increase in your sales; which exactly what consultative selling is all about.

So how do you become more of a consultative seller?

Be Curious

The best way to sell to anyone is to ask plenty of questions and to remain curious.

Let's revise the doctor analogy and think back to the last time you went to your doctors. The chances are you did not walk into the consultation room and have the doctor take one look at you and proceed to trying to offer you a medicine that is on promotion at that moment in time in an effort to help him or her meet their prescribing targets:

"Ahh, I know what you will like! This new Trazapan Potion is on offer right now and is guaranteed to make you better!"

It doesn't work like that does it? Doctors ask questions. They probe. They test. They ensure that they understand your needs and desires way before they offer you something.

It is no similar to the work of a detective either, or a Police Officer conducting an interview. When a crime occurs, an officer must keep an open mind, look for clues, seek out witness and ultimately ask the right questions, to the right people, at the right time. In doing so, the officer or detective can truly understand what has gone on and the best way forward to rectify the situation.

If you start to ask your prospect and customers more questions, no different to how a doctor or a detective were to, then not only will you find yourself developing strong business relationships with your prospects but you will also see that your life as a sales person becomes easier because all you have to do is to offer the best solution to your prospects problem.

Understand

It is all well and good asking questions but be sure to understand your buyer's needs. Do not be afraid to ask further questions to help you clarify, and do not feel embarrassed to admit you need time to research or think of a solution for their needs; this will only help you to develop a stronger rapport.

The majority of the time, your buyer may not fully know what he or she actually wants. By being a consultant, and by working hard to understand your buyer, you will be able to guide your prospect through the sales process and find the right solution to the problem.

One of the most effective ways to truly understand what your prospect is telling you to repeat to your prospect the statements they make. Simply saying terms like:

"So from what you have told me so far, you are currently facing problems with XYZ and you are looking for a way to fix these problems."

Or

"Just let me repeat that all back to you so I can make sure I have understood everything you have told me and then I can look to see what solutions I can offer."

Once you have truly understood what your prospect has told you all you then have to do is push forward with your solutions and ask for the sale!

Mirror Your Prospect

Everyone is different. Not two of your customers are the same and the way one person communicates and does business can be completely different to another person.

With this in mind it is so important that you learn to adapt your pitch for each presentation or conversation you have and you mirror your buyer. Just because a certain script or a certain way of talking to someone worked for some sales does not mean it will work for everyone.

Mirroring is the simple behaviour where you will look to imitate the speech patterns, attitudes, body language and gestures of your prospect. Although this happens often unconsciously and normally goes very unnoticed, by purposefully mirroring your prospect you will see that you will develop a strong rapport with people much quicker than normal. You see, when we notice that our actions and gestures are being mirrored then it allows us the chance to feel a higher sense of engagement and belonging within the conversation. This could be simple things such as mirroring the tone, or volume of your prospects voice. Or even the way they are sitting or standing. It could even be matching the pace in which they are eating or drinking. The more observant you can be the more clues you will pick up on how you should act.

Take the time to care for each and every single one of your prospects, treat them as individuals and you will soon find that you will become a consultative seller in next to no time!

The Need to Follow Up

I have the honour and the privilege to work with a lot of sales people and business owners from around the globe and I love being able to help them to turn their sales fortunes around.

I sit down with them, listen to their sales processes. I observe their sales methods and pick up on what they are doing right, and perhaps what they are doing wrong.

And I can tell you now that there is one common theme that tends to occur with those that aren't making enough sales and those that are struggling to close enough deals:

They are not following up enough with their

prospects.

Many people are pitching their product or service, perhaps even getting so far within the process to be quoting their prospect certain fees – but then they never hear anything back from them. So they sit back and wait. They wait some more. Before you know it two months have gone by and they have heard nothing from their once interested customer.

And when you confront these individuals and ask why they have not followed up with their prospects the excuses start coming out:

"Ahh, they were just time wasters."

Or, "they were tyre kickers".

The amount of excuses that sales people come out with when someone has not bought is highly excessive and does not get anyone anywhere. And yet it happens a lot.

Some, and only some, sales people and business owners will speak to that prospect again and ask once again for the sale. Or ask for the next steps within the sales process; and it is here where the most success occurs.

The follow up is the most crucial stage to the buying or sales process.

I cannot stress this enough; if you are not following up with your prospect on more than one occasion you are rarely going to get the sale. I know I harp on about it a lot but following up with your prospect or customer within the sales process is a sure-fire way to help you to increase your sales in a short space of time.

One of the biggest obstacles to overcome when selling a product or service is trust. Without trust a sale cannot occur. And yet we live in a messy world full of 'buy me' messages with no follow through. Answer truthfully; how many times a week do you receive an email or LinkedIn message from someone trying to sell you goods or services – and then to never hear from that business or person again. They could perhaps have the number one product you need at that time, and for all intents and purposes you could be tempted to buy it; but because this person has never developed a relationship with you, or developed any trust, you decide to not go ahead. The more points of contact you introduce into the sales process the more points that go towards relationship building. The more trust building the better!

What we have to remember is that your product or service may not be your prospects number one concern right now either. Think back to one of our earlier chapters about thinking about the bigger picture. The proposal you have sent over to your prospect may just be a minuscule part of their current mindset and their life right now and they may have a million and one other things to deal with; you may think you are not forgettable and that the thing you are selling is the most important thing in the World however the truth is that you may just have wandered to the back of your prospects head.

This is why following up with your prospect is so vital. It develops trust. It proves to your prospect that you are not just a flash in the pan and it proves that you truly want their business and you also have every faith that your product or service is just exactly what your prospect needs to improve their life. It also keeps you in the forefront of your prospects mind. Following up acts as a gentle reminder that you are there for your prospect; it reminds them you want their business and you can remind them how much your product or service will benefit them.

So how many times should you follow up with your prospect? Once? Twice?

I always say no less than seven to 12 times, and as up to as many as it takes to get an answer. Recent statistics prove that 80% of all sales occur after five points of contact so it makes perfect sense to contact them no less than five times. And until you hear a definite 'no', there is no point in stopping contact. You cannot mind read, and you cannot make excuses on behalf of your prospect as to why they do not want to buy from you, or why they have not contacted you. So, until you hear the valid reasons as to why they don't want to buy – keep going!

It is important to mix up the way you follow up with your prospect too. Let's use a very basic example to help illustrate my point:

Let's say I send a proposal via email for sales training to someone whom has approached me. I send that email on day one with the proposal attached. I wait it out for several days and hear nothing back. On day five I email them again asking for their feedback. Once again I hear nothing. So on day ten I email them again. Upon hearing nothing again I just close off the opportunity in my CRM or on my sales board and I move on to the next one. But I never get in contact with that prospect and I never truly understand the reason why they didn't want to buy my service.

Do you think the above scenario is good practice? Of course it isn't. There are multiple ways in which you could contact your prospect, and you should try all of them;

Phone calls, emails, direct messages on social media, face to face visits and direct mail account for some of the many methods of contact available to you; so use them all. If a prospect doesn't reply to your email, call them up. If they aren't available for a call, send them a hard letter through the post. If they still do not respond, turn up at their office. This may seem confrontational to some but it really does not have to be. You can go to the shop, buy some doughnuts and turn up at their office unannounced whilst stating you were just in the area. If you truly want their business and you really want to do business with someone then be sure to go above and beyond and prove this to them. The more times you make contact in a multitude of ways the better the chance you will have of either making the sales, or understanding why they have decided to not shop with you. And by understanding this you can either propose a different service or package or you can seek some different referrals.

I get asked many times about the rate in which you should follow up, and how often you should follow up. For me, there is no definitive answer. You should always be wary of becoming too needy, and being too forceful with your prospect of course and some of your customers will want to be followed up with more often than others. From my own experience, I generally say to follow up on the initial proposal or quote within 3-5 days. This will give your prospect time to think things over and will give them a chance to read through everything properly. As time goes on, you can afford to leave a longer period of time between follow ups. So by the 7th or 8th contact you might be able to afford to wait 14 days or so. However one way to understand this better is to just ask your prospect and set the ground rules. During the presentation or during the sales conversation all you have to ask is something along the lines of:

"Mrs Jones, once I have sent over the proposal I of course would like to follow up with you to make sure it all makes sense and I have included everything you wanted. How long should I leave it with you for, and which method of contact would you prefer me to make with you?"

This not only sets the ground rules but will also allow you the chance to play by the rules set out by your prospect; this way they cannot moan that you are chasing them too often or neglecting them in any shape or form.

Try it in your sales process from now on. Do not just send out a proposal and hope you hear back from your prospect and don't just leave the buying process in their hands.

Then don't just send one email asking your prospect if they have had a chance to look over your proposal or just one direct message on LinkedIn, or a text. Show and demonstrate to your prospect that you care. Show them that you deserve their business. And most of all, prove to your prospect that you are there for them and that you are not just going to vanish once the sale is made.

Look to close the sale but open the relationship.

List Objections Early

Every sales process is going to feature plenty of objections and as a sales person or a business owner you are going to hear a lot of objections. But there is one simple way you can reduce the negative impact an objection may have on your sales presentation.

We have already covered objections thoroughly earlier on in this book so you should already be quite clued up about objections and should understand them already. But if it has been a few days since you last read that chapter, let's go over them briefly once again.

In your sales cycle you are going to get to a stage when you attempt to close the sale; or you in fact try to ask the customer to buy whatever it is you are offering; whether it be a product or a service. An objection will likely be used as a response to your offer and is simply a way of objecting whatever it is you have proposed. Objections come in all forms of guises however will more than likely be a reason why the prospect does not want to buy from you. Perhaps you are too expensive. Or they feel that your service is too far away and not local enough for them. Or perhaps they have not fully understood what it is you are selling. You may hear things like; "I cannot afford it." Or "I need to think about it." Once again, if you want to revisit objections in more depth I would recommend going back over the earlier chapter in this book.

So for now, instead of thinking about objections as such, let's start to think about perhaps the flaws in your product or service.

One thing you must become an expert in doing is critiquing your own product or service and thinking of the objections that may come up in a sales presentation and the things that might put someone off buying from you. This is where good role playing sessions with a colleague, and manager or your partner can really help you out. Find out and think of all of the negatives that you can as to why someone will not want your offer, and write them down. Or maybe use real examples from real sales scenarios; things your real potential customers have told you. Next, write down all of the reasons why the objection should not matter and how you can get past the negatives. Think of yourself as a political spin doctor at this stage. So, for example, if you were to hear;

"We just like to buy local produce."

You can respond with; "Yes, I completely agree with you. I understand we are based a long way from you however we have invested a lot of money to ensure that food miles are kept to a minimum and that all of our transport links are well managed. Plus, all of our ingredients are locally sourced to our factory to help to keep these food miles down."

Or have you ever heard of this one?

"You are at the top end of our budget."

You could then respond with; "Sure, we hear that a lot. So to counter act this we provide a lot of extra support that our competitors will not. So you get full access to our marketing channels and we also provide extra support for a longer period of time. Ultimately you will have me as your main point of contact so you never have to waste time with a call centre or anything like that; which wills ave you a lot of time and money in the long run."

Once you have recognised all of these objections and potential flaws with your product and planned out responses to them, be sure to practice them and learn them so that when called upon you can just reel them off nice and simply.

There is no doubt in my mind that every single product or service out there has some form of flaw or potential negative aspect to it so don't sit there and thing that you are perfect and flawless!

My other advice for this important chapters is for you to bring up your objections yourself in your sales presentation. Instead of waiting for an objection to come your way which your prospect may be thinking about and harming their ability to listen to you, pre-empt the objection first:

"Now, we understand that we are a premium range, and that is why we offer extra marketing and technical support."

"As an upcoming brand, we understand you perhaps have your reservations about buying from us. However, to counter this we offer a guarantee on all purchases and to develop a trust and a relationship between us we would like to offer you a 'sale or return' proposal."

By recognising the points that people may object to your sales proposal, you will be better equipped to push the sale through and to overcome the objection. And offering the objection up front, on your own terms, will stop any good sales flow later on throughout the process. It is like putting all of your cards on the table that cannot trip you up later on. Sure, you can sit back and hope that your prospect doesn't think of these flaws but if they do it is automatically going to put you on the back foot and will affect the flow of your conversation.

Be upfront, be honest, and be ahead of the game!

What are you Selling?

I remember back in my early days of selling when I was fresh, young and green my manager took me to one side and said;
"Don't sell the features, sell the benefits."

I am confident you have heard that term too. The idea of selling benefits over features has been around for a very long time; and if you haven't heard of the term consciously I am sure somewhere deep within you that you will be aware of the difference. However if this is completely new to you, here is a brief overview:

Every product or service has a feature. A feature is a distinctive attribute of a product or service. This feature is 'what it is' or 'what it does'. Each feature, then has a benefit. A reason as to why your customer will profit or will gain from that said product or service.

So for example, let's say you open up a coffee shop with free WiFi. The feature in this example is the free WiFi aspect of your business. The benefit of this is that your customers can work, study or chat to friends and family whilst enjoying their coffee. Out of the two terms here; 'free WiFi' or the ability to 'work and socialise', do you think sounds the most appealing?

Or let's look at the original iPod. When it was first released, the key selling point was that you could; "Fit 1000 songs in your pocket". This is the BENEFIT of the iPod. The Feature was that it offered 1GB of storage. Now, if Steve Jobs had gone around selling the feature of the iPod do you think so many people would have been aware as to what 1GB meant, and how it would impact them? Most probably not.

If you look around, you at every advertisement or marketing copy you can lay your eyes on we are led by the benefits of the product or service; it is the benefit that makes the customer wants to buy.

You see, when we see how a product or service can benefit our lives or our business then we tend to develop a stronger emotional response to it. This in turn develops a desire for us to own it. And if you think back to the our earlier chapter about Objections you will remember that prospects having a lack of desire in our products or services will lead them to not want to buy it. So with all of this in mind, the more you sell the benefits of your product or service the greater chance your audience will want and desire it!

Is a financial advisor really selling financial advise? Or are they selling a stable and more fruitful future for one's family?

Is a Virtual Assistant really selling email and diary support? Or are they selling the concept of free time?

Is a cleaner selling you the chance for a clean home? Or are they selling the ability for you to come home and to relax whilst again saving valuable time?

You can see the point I am getting to here.

If you can utilise the idea of selling the benefits over the features in your sales pitch and even within your marketing materials then you will see a much better rate of selling in your business and for that I am sure. No one really cares that your shop is open for 24 hours a day. But they do care that they can pick up a pint of milk at 5am when they want to pour their cereal. No one really cares that your IT company offers unlimited phone support. But your customer does care that when their computer breaks during the write up of an important proposal with a deadline that they can call you for support straight away. Even the gas bill that is posted through your door every quarter isn't a bill for gas; it is the ability to heat your house, your food and your water.

I want you to take a break for minute from this book and to make some notes on the features and benefits of your business and the products or services you sell. Think long and hard about all of the things you claim you can offer to your customers and all of the things your products and services do, and then note down how these can benefit your customers. If you find that you are not talking about the benefits so much in your presentations and marketing materials then now is your chance to mix that up and implement changes!

Selling the benefits increases a buyers emotional response to a product, in-turn generating more desire!

Taking this one step further, I encourage all of my clients to think deeply about what it is they are really selling.

No one ever in the history of man-kind has woken up and decided that they want to buy a spade! You wouldn't walk into B&Q and think to yourself; "you know what? Today is the day I treat myself to a spade!" But, the likelihood is that when buying a spade, you actually want a hole. The same could be said about a drill. You aren't really buying a drill. You are buying the ability to create a hole. Once again, once you recognise this and understand what it is you are really selling the ability to sell becomes so much easier.

Does that all make sense?

Once you crack the code of what you really sell, selling becomes so much easier!

So, I urge you; go away and look at your product or service and think about what you really are selling. Are you selling a photography service, or are you selling memories? Are you selling a mobile phone, or are you selling the ability to communicate? Are you selling business cards, or are you selling a marketing opportunity?

What are you really selling?

Captivate Your Audience

Get your prospects attention, and KEEP IT!

In the earlier chapter about presentations, we briefly mentioned how you should look to captivate your audience and how you should keep their attention. Well ladies and gentleman, this here is the chapter you have been waiting for!

Have you ever listened to someone waffle on, pitch to you, and talk to you to the extent where you faze out and start thinking about what you have planned for dinner? Or where your mind wanders away to a beautiful beach?

It happens a lot unfortunately, and the chances are we have all caused someone to drift off and away into their own bubble. But as a sales person that is the last thing you want. You need to keep your customer, or your prospects focussed on you so that you can sell them the solution to their problems.

Ever heard of the Cocktail Party Phenomenon? You have more than likely experienced it without even knowing it. You will be at a party in a crowded room having a conversation with someone when suddenly from the other side of the room you hear your name mentioned in conversation. You then carry on listening to that other conversation and lose the chain of the original conversation you were having. Before you know it you are just nodding and agreeing to what the person in front of you is saying without truly understanding what on earth they are going on about.

This phenomenon occurs because us humans cannot process two conversations at once.

So how can we grab the attention of those we are talking to, and how do we keep it?

A lot of early sales training, and even guidance on how to write sales copy, centred around the AIDA principle; Attention, Interest, Desire, Action. The AIDA principle is an absolute saviour for when it comes to writing anything from emails, to LinkedIn posts, to social media posts, and even sales copy for leaflets amongst other things. Once you have got a grasp of the AIDA principle and understand it to it's fullest sales writing becomes an awful lot easier. AIDA is used to describe the stages, or steps perhaps, that occur when a consumer or your prospect first becomes aware of your brand, your service or your product all the way through the pipeline until that prospect signs on the dotted line and becomes a fully-fledged customer. So, if you were to look at it a little more broken down you will see that at the Attention phase the customer is becoming aware of you, your company and your product. This can be through advertising or could be from a visit from you as a sales person or perhaps even a telephone call from yourself. The next stage is to develop Interest in the product or service. So, at this stage, you are starting to generate a little steam. A little momentum perhaps. You are able to demonstrate to your prospect the benefits of your service or product and how it can benefit their life or their circumstances. Next comes the key stage to this section of the book; the Desire. Without desire we will never want for anything in our lives. A desire is a very strong feeling we get when we either want something, or we wait and wish for something to happen. To me, and the way I look at it is like this; to desire something you can see you in your minds eye something that you want. You can pretty much touch it, experience it and imagine yourself being a part of something. We are going to look closely at desire in just one moment, however to finish off the AIDA explanation; A is referring getting your prospect to act upon something. That could perhaps be a purchase. Or signing up to a new monthly agreement or subscribing to your email marketing list. The action is the close. The final hooray.

So, there we have it - perhaps the swiftest explanation ever to the AIDA principal. Be sure to memorise it though if you have never seen it or heard of it before. It can be a very useful tool for all of you marketers, advertisers and business owners out there. Sales people too might I add. If you can use the AIDA principal in your sales proposals, pitches and speeches you will find that you can write them with a more focussed mindset and will keep you on track.

If you cannot captivate your audience, you will fail to firstly grab the attention of your prospect, getting your prospects Interest and then develop their interest in your business or service. Don't get caught out!

Get In Early

My attention span is about 3 seconds long, however according to Microsoft the average person starts to lose interest after 8 seconds. Not long at all is it? Keep your message short, keep it to the point and do not waste your prospects valuable time with idol chit chat or blurred facts. Get to the point and get to it fast.

Stop Talking About Yourself

Quit telling your prospect about your business and your life. Put simply, they do not care.

Talk to your prospect about THEIR problems and ask them questions to figure out how you can work together. Remember, the more questions you asks the better! Only talk about your brand and your services when it is relevant to their problems.

Focus On One Thing

This world is getting cluttered with information. We are surrounded by adverts, technology and distractions. Just like the Cocktail Party Phenomenon scenario earlier; don't allow your message to get lost in a crowded room.

Keep your points solid and only divulge them one at a time. Try to avoid going off on random tangents that lead nowhere and leave your audience feeling lost and unable to follow.

Don't Be A Bore

Have some fun for Gods sake. You are a human being right?
Not a machine. No matter what you are saying, no matter what message you are portraying, be sure to make it enjoyable. Don't become known for your boring Powerpoint presentations and your 'yawn inducing pitches'. Make people smile - you will be remembered for that. Humour can certainly go a long way in business and in sales. I am not suggesting that you need to turn your pitches and presentations into full on comedic sketches. However show some personality and try to make people smile. Remember; people buy from people, and the more of your own beautiful and wonderful personality you can portray the better the chances you will have to sell more!

Keep It Intimate

It doesn't matter if you are talking with one person, or presenting to 100 people. Keep it personal. Have a conversation with your audience and refrain from talking at or to your audience. Once again you will only push them away and lose focus.

A good conversation will be remembered well above a spoken word or a preaching session.

Handling Your Competition

As a business owner, or even as a sales professional you will be well aware of your competition. In fact, even as part of business plans you are expected to take a lot of your time to research your competition, see what they do, how they do it, and how you can stand apart from them.

Even as a sales professional or entrepreneur you will have come across your competition at some stage. You will know exactly what they do, how they do it and why they do it.

Despite all of this recognition and research being given to our competition, we are never given any guidance on handling business competition. Nor are we ever taught how to act towards the competition.

In my eyes, the way in which we talk about our competition and handle them can stand us apart.

Handling business competition, or how you handle your own feelings towards your competition is a personal choice. No one can ever tell you how you should feel about your competition, but, it's good to have a reality check from time to time. It is also terribly important to make the decision to not publicly let your feelings known about them, and we will come on to why shortly.

You will never escape competition. And in my eyes, that is a very positive thing. Without business competition, you will never try to better yourself or better your company's offerings. You will become far too relaxed and complacent. No different to the number one goalkeeper at a football club. If the number one doesn't have someone trying to better them, trying to grab hold of that number one spot then it is very easy to become complacent and slip off the boil.

It is very easy to have emotions of jealousy, anger, hatred, or even fear for your competition and your competitors and I think many of you will join me in saying that all of these feelings are very normal and should not be ashamed of. It is easy to have these feelings slip in to our minds but it is important to remain positive about our competition and be thankful for what they do and what they offer. Especially when talking to prospects.

One thing that should never happen when handling business competition is to talk bad of them to others. You should never 'slag off' or speak poorly of your competition

- especially in your sales pitch or sales presentation. And most certainly not on any form of social media channels. It is so easy when presenting to your prospect to speak poorly of your competition in the hope that they will be put off buying from them instead of you. Imagine a scenario in which your prospect admits to you that they have also been in talks with your closest competitors. Do you think you will come off well to your prospect if you start saying anything like these comments?

"Oh you should not buy from them! They will only rip you off. We have seen it so many times."

"You don't want to buy from them if you can help it. Con-artists!"

"Yeah they always charge cheaper prices but that is only because their work is horrendous! The quality of work they offer is just poor!"

Some of these statements may be similar to what you have used in the past? Or perhaps you have heard them from others? Either way, they are pointless and should never be brought up in a sales presentation. You see, when you start to become known as someone who talks badly about others, it does not give you a good reputation and people will become wary to do business with you; if you are so happy to slag others off, how easy is it for you to slag them off?

If you feel that you need to drag down someone else to only raise yourself or to try to make yourself seem better then it is safe to say whatever it is you are selling just is inadequate. It's like a bullies mentality.

Belittling others will only become a reflection upon yourself.

The way I see it is this: your competition is there for a reason. They have had their own successes and must have done some great work for them to be known by your prospect. So show them the respect they deserve. If you are dealing with a situation where you are up against your competition, remain gracious at all times. Show your competition the respect they deserve.

On the other side of this is the fact that if you show any ill-respect to your prospects choice of previous supplier, or potential supplier you are not going to come across well to your prospect. They could have been serviced by your competition for several years and you are now mocking them for that decision? Or perhaps your prospects cousin is the MD of your competition. You simply never know.

Always err on the side on the side of caution when it comes to talking about your competition. If you cannot say anything nice, don't say anything at all. I think Thumper said that to his good friend Bambi. Sure - you do not have to shower them with praise, but you should be willing and humble enough to say; "Yes they do good work!" or "I have heard of them before, it sounds like they are doing well!"

So when it comes to handling business competition, don't be a jealous fool. Remain humble and show respect. Your prospect does not want to hear you slagging anyone off. And if you feel you need to; up your game!

I assure you that by remaining polite and courteous towards your competitors, especially in front of your customers and prospects then you will be seen as a better offering and a better person. This will earn you a status in society that could be unrivalled. Your prospects will have a new found confidence in you as they can recognise that you are not worried or fazed by your competitors which in turn will grant you a higher level of trust.

Of course - if you ever need assistance on your sales pitch then be sure to make contact with the Paragon Sales Solutions team whom will be more than willing and happy to get you the results you deserve.

Keep Prospecting

A lot of sales people and business owners spend a lot of their time and energy on closing sales, and closing deals. They also preach and believe that you should 'Always Be Closing' and that the sales closing phase is the most important aspect of the sales process. They set targets, they brag to their friends and peers about how good of a closer they are, and even jobs and careers are sometimes lost over how few sales are closed in a set amount of time.

Closing a sale is of course very important; without doing so you are not going to turnover any money. We all know that. But what would happen if we turned this whole theory on its head?

The amount of people at the start of your sales

process, or at the top of your sales funnel some will call it, is far more important than what happens at the end of that process. In theory, the more people you are getting into your sales cycle, and the more people you are prospecting with then the larger amount of people that will be there available to close further down the line. Not only that, but what happens when you close all of your open deals without spending any time of focus on prospecting? You dry up. You soon lose a nice long chain of people all waiting to be closed and you simply have to start again.

Allow me to explain this via a parable.

A farmer buys a new plot of land. This land is big enough to plant 1000 pieces of corn. The farmer goes out and starts to plant the seeds. Before long, the farmer has planted all 1000 seeds and lets nature take its course. As the plants grow, the farmer goes out and nurtures the young plants. He waters them, feeds them, takes out the dead or weak plants and stops any weeds from growing in between the rows. In no time at all, 500 of the plants are ready to be harvested. Unfortunately, as this parable is set in the olden days without any machinery he has to do it by hand. He sets out to collect the 500 pieces of corn and removes the now unneeded plants. As he does so, the land becomes bare once again with many empty spaces. A month later, the rest of the corn is ready, and the farmer once again goes out to collect his corn. Now, the field is empty and bare.

The next day he speaks with his farmer neighbour and boasts about how after general wastage, he was able to gather 800 pieces of corn. The neighbour laughs.

"Just 800 pieces?" He asks. "I managed to take in 1800 pieces. And my land is smaller than yours"

"But how did you manage that?" Asks the farmer.

"Well, you need to learn; once space appears in your field you need to lay down new seed and make the most of the season. The more seeds you sow, the more corn you can harvest at the end of the growing cycle."

I am no farming expert and please don't criticise me for not understanding fully how corn grows. However, the point I am trying to make here is this; if you focus so much on your customers whom are at the end of your sales cycle, and those that you are trying to close, then you will soon forget to start talking to new prospects. If you are not out there planting seeds and filling up your sales pipeline then you eventually get to a point where you are drying up and you have no one to close.

The more seeds you sow, the more you can harvest.

Try to think about this when you are out and about being a super sales person. Sure, closing sales is vital, and is certainly something that you need to be doing and a whole chapter will be included in this book solely on closing sales. But do not ever focus on closing sales so much that you forget to prospect for new business and forget to plant new seeds.

So with all of that being said, how should you go about prospecting? What does prospecting mean? And what activities should you be conducting to ensure you are prospecting as efficiently as possible?

Now, prior to contrary belief, prospecting for new business does not mean scrolling through LinkedIn, Facebook, Instagram and Twitter in the hope of finding someone wanting to do business with you. Prospecting is a task that requires time, dedication and skill. It means you getting out there, setting yourself targets (no different to the targets you would make for closing sales) and making those all important connections and contacts to allow you to fill your sales pipeline up.

As we have already mentioned and talked about in this book, activities such as social selling, networking, and speaking events make for a great way to prospect for new business and to find new people to talk to.

Here are five simple resources and ideas that you can use starting from today that will give you plenty of new prospects to talk to and will give you plenty of chances for more sales.

Old Clients

Every single business, no matter how big or small has a database of old clients all of whom have used your products or services before. These should be fairly easily accessible and stored securely on your businesses computer systems (in accordance with GDPR of course) and will certainly give you plenty of opportunities to redevelop fresh new business.

The people in these databases are an ideal crowd to sell to; they already are qualified, and there should be a relationship already developed with them. So get on the phone, re-invigorate that business relationship and see if there is more business to be had!

Even better, go out and visit them! Load yourself up with some cakes and treats, and spend the day going around visiting them. And never worry if these are past clients from years ago in which you personally have never had any contact with. These people will have heard of your company in some form or another and this will give you strong, sturdy ground to allow you to start your very own relationship with them.

Your Circles

I bet my bottom dollar that you have a circle of friends and associates around you that you have had some form of contact with in the past; be it at a networking event, or just in passing at a business exhibition. These could be people whom you have had a general conversation with, gathered their business cards and then just let their details gather dust in a draw in the office.

Now is the time to start some crucial conversations! It is amazing how when we start to look for people to sell to we soon realise that there are plenty of people close to us that could make for the most perfect client.

Your personal circles and your network could be the key to your next big sale.

Cold-Calling

Cold-Calling is not as scary as you may think (and if you are really worried, the team here at Paragon Sales Solutions will be more than happy to help you!)

But really, cold-calling is still the number one way to find new leads. You can start a conversation, develop a desire and start developing a strong business relationship with real businesses.

We have already discussed great detail throughout this book how the phone still makes a massive impact within sales and is a tool that should not be overlooked.

You can either source some business data though a data broker and call through a list of your ideal target audience, or you could simply search for the details of all the businesses on the trading estate next to you. No matter what; don't make excuses and set yourself targets!

Do not neglect the telephone when it comes to your prospecting time.

Asking for referrals

Coming back to what we said earlier about your own circles and networks, this can also be extended out into your clients and customers too! Everyone whom has ever done business with you will have their own network of people who will potentially want to do business with you. And with your client on side, you could be given a referral that leads to your biggest sale.

Remember, we all like to buy from people we trust; and that is why when a friend recommends a certain service, or puts in a good word for someone, we already develop a stronger sense of trust.

You do not have to make a big song or a dance about this, and although sometimes it is nice to offer a referral fee or gift if the budget allows, sometimes all you have to do is pick up the phone and ask:

"Hey Mary, listen; you have been using our services now for 2 months and from everything you have told me it has worked wonders for you! Is there anyone that you know personally whom you feel would also benefit from this?"

If you do not ask, you do not get! The worst that can happen is that they say no, and aren't able to refer anyone. But for all you know, this person could hand you their little black book and circle ten names whom could be your next sale!

So call through your current clients and see if they know anyone who could use your products or services!

Add on Sales

And whilst you are calling through or visiting your current clients and customers, is there anything else they could potentially buy from you? Do you have any other products or services you feel they could benefit from? Every business has extras that can further benefit our customers.

Even McDonalds employ this tactic; and it works so well! What happens when you visit one of their restaurants to order a burger? Their team are trained to ask:

"Do you want fries with that?"

This simple question will never upset anyone, never offend, and yet will offer their customers the chance to say 'yes' which in turn, I am sure, has added £millions on to their yearly revenue.

Keep your radar open and look for additional sales that can be had.

Ultimately, we all need to prospect to see our sales pipeline full up full of potential deals all waiting to be had; if we do not prospect for new business, we will always struggle to meet our targets.

Staying Healthy

To be a sales person, you do not really need any training, and you do not really need to look after your health; both physical and mental. The same can very much be said for business owners and other professionals too.

However, that being said, to be a top performing sales professional you need to stay on top of your sales training, keep abreast of new techniques and skills, and to ensure that you keep on top of both your physical and your mental health. By implementing these elements, you will see an increase in your sales that will only benefit you, your business, and your family.

Think of yourself as a professional athlete. The moment you stop training, stop eating well and start ingesting every alcohol and drug on the planet then you will soon start to drop down into the amateur leagues, or even worse.

I have been there myself personally; I do like to keep physically fit and yet from time to time in the past I have I let this slip. I let myself overwork and I over indulge in the wrong kinds of foods, exercise less and I eventually put on far too much weight! Normally this is because I am reaching for a bag of Haribo when I am driving to my next meeting, or just snacking whilst at my desk. But not only is my physical appearance affected by this nonchalant approach to my health, but it really affects my performance too. This is why I have invested in standing up desks (to ensure I am not sitting down too long and I am encouraging blood flow), but I also invest a minimum of one hour a day to pure, solid exercise.

Now, I could waffle on for pages about why you too should think about investing in your own health, but I thought it best I introduce someone to you; Ben Driver.

Ben Driver is a Personal Trainer by trade, but is also an incredible copywriter and content creator too. So incredible in fact, Ben has recently joined the Paragon Sales Solutions team as our expert copywriter.

The reason I have asked Ben to write this chapter is simple; he knows his stuff!

You only have to take one look at him to know that he trains hard, and yet has a sensible approach to eating and exercise - the man has a body like a God and yet isn't afraid to demolish a cheeseboard and a bottle of red wine!

But not only that, with Ben's passion for sales and marketing too, who better than to tell you all you need to know about staying fit and healthy, and how doing so can increase your sales.

So, over to you Ben...

Why Diet And Exercise Is The Foundation Of Selling

In a quest to better your sales ability you likely focus on high ROI tasks. You know, those tasks that are the most important things you need to do, they give you the biggest bang for your buck in terms of time invested versus their outcome.

Now when you think of the biggest ROI tasks, your mind generally jumps straight to the direct stuff: writing sales copy, marketing, building customer rapport.

Rarely though, does self-care come under the ROI umbrella.

Yet self-care is one of, if not THE biggest ROI task you can possibly focus on in selling.

There is an 'energy' you give off when you don't look after yourself. You can't sell at your full potential if you're feeling sluggish and have no drive.

Think of Beethoven,. Sure you could learn to play some his music, but you will never be able to replicate it fully because there is something that is translated about a person's mood, state and emotion when they put themselves out there.

Which is the same in selling.

To give you some perspective, let me tell you a story:

A few months back I was sat down writing an email to my list of subscribers. This is one of my highest ROI tasks and generally this is where the majority of my sales comes from, second to in-person consultations.

Now usually when I'm selling or building a relationship with a potential customer, whether it's written or in person, my mood needs to be great and my energy high.

You'll have likely noticed this before, but when you're in a bad mood and your energy is low, even when you think you're managing to 'fake it' your customer can tell a mile off.

Which is what happened to me.

I was so involved in my business that all of my high ROI tasks did not involve keeping my mind and body healthy at all.

They were all external tasks that I needed to get done - so I neglected my training and my diet suffered.

This then translated into my selling.

So, as I mentioned before, I was sat writing my usual email and while I thought I was 'faking' it and pushing through my low mood and lack of energy, I was in fact sabotaging my selling ability.

My usual personality-laden and funny email that tends to do very well actually came out as completely bitter.

In my mind the email looked nothing out of the ordinary but it wasn't until I started getting replies back that I knew I was damaging myself.

"Ben I usually love your emails, but are you having a bad morning?" "This one missed the mark, nevermind, maybe next time."

It was at this point I realised that setting some time aside every day to look after my nutrition and do some exercise was probably the most important thing I could do for myself and my business.

I find that when I'm eating well and exercising daily that my sales performance, creativity and mood increases.

The effects snowball and that's why it's so crucial to make sure you have this covered. If you eat like crap and never exercise then you really are, excuse the pun, selling yourself short.

So, to get you started:

4 Fitness Tips That Will Help Increase Your Sales Performance And Mood Without You Having To Spend Hours In The Gym

(Note: At first you may struggle to justify taking time out of your day to focus on these but just know that this will have a huge impact on your performance if you remain consistent and implement immediately)

#1 - Stay hydrated.

Yes this may seem super obvious but - drink more water.

A lot of sales professionals I've worked with tend to live off of coffee and usually forget to drink water throughout the day.

There are plenty of reusable water bottle options and if you really struggle to remember to drink water you can even set a timer on your phone.

The side-effects of being dehydrated on their own show you just how much your performance can be affected:

Lethargy, headache, dizziness, weakness in muscles - just to name a few.

#2 - The 80/20 rule

Life is about moderation and balance.

The majority of your food should be whole and nutritious. You should focus on good protein sources (fish, meat, eggs), good fat sources (nuts, avocado, olive oil), moderate amounts of carbohydrates (rice, potato, oats) and plenty of vegetables.

This should be the focus of your diet (80%). Not only will this make you feel fuller, your energy levels will be more consistent and you won't get those slumps and spikes of energy that you're likely used to when you forget to eat or eat processed foods.

After your base is covered you can then use the other 20% to pretty much eat what you want.

#3 Learn to salsa dance

Unless you actually want to learn to salsa dance, that's not actually the tip here.

The point of this is that I want you to pick some form of exercise that you enjoy doing.

You'll read a ton of information online about what the absolute best form of exercise is, whether it's weight training, running, cycling, dancing it all tends to be bias to what the author prefers. It also means you spend more time researching the best activity to do rather than actually doing something.

The important thing here is that you pick something that takes you away from your work for 30-60 minutes and raises your heart rate.

This will burn a load of calories, get you fitter and is a great mental break from your work. Plus I tend to get a lot of my ideas when I step out of my business for a while.

So go for a walk, lift some weights or join a class - just get out of your comfort zone, out of the office and get moving.

#4 Count sheep.

Get some sleep.

I get that you're a machine that can work for 21 hours a day and you only need 3 hours of sleep but no one can keep this up forever.

The thing is, sleep and rest are vital in regulating your mood and energy - making you perform better.

When it comes to sleep, while you need a good amount, quality tends to trump quantity.

So if you really do struggle to get the hours in, then improving your quality can make an immediate impact. Here are some tips you can implement straight away:

> - Stop using screens at least an hour before bed (blue light interrupts your ability to produce melatonin).

> - Don't allow light in your bedroom (black-out blinds or a sleeping mask can help)

- No caffeine after lunch (the half-life of caffeine can be around 6 hours which means it'll likely still be in your system when you go to sleep if you drink it too late in the day)

- Brain dump before you go to bed (As a busy salesperson your mind is constantly active, write down everything you need to do the next day in a notepad to make sure you don't think about it when you lie down)

Want to learn more about Ben, and to find out how he can help you in your quest for sales and business fitness, be sure to check him out online!

bendriverfitness.co.uk

Owning up to Mistakes

Let's face it; mistooks happen from time to time.

We are all human after all, and mistakes are going to happen. And these mistakes can be the failings of either an individual or a whole system and process. But there is no denying it; accidents and mistakes will happen.

In your sales career or your business career you too are going to mistakes that are going to have an impact on your prospects or your customer. You might misquote someone. You might miss an important delivery date. You might have forgotten to mention some crucial details in the product or service offering. It happens.

It is so important as a sales professional to be ready to stand up to these mistakes and to get ready for any backlash that may occur. You see, as a sales person the likelihood is that you didn't deliver the services of the goods personally and you might not have manufactured them or arranged the pricing; you just acted as the person in the middle. Allowing for the transaction to flow from one to the next. However, the likelihood is that you will feel the full brunt from your customer.

Why?

Simple. You are the face of the company you represent. You are the sales representative after all. So, whenever your customer thinks of your company, they are going to think of you. You are also the voice of the company; the one whom has negotiated and conversed the whole sale from start to finish. You are the most personable, relatable part of the business and it is with that good reason that you may be put in the spotlight when things go bad.

But this is a good thing.

First of all, if a client comes to you first with some form of complaint or issue, this means that they trust you. They trust that you have the solution to the problem and you can help out in their time of need. They like you so much that they have turned to you for help.

With that in mind; do not start to pass the blame. It can be so easy whenever anything goes wrong during any sale or transaction to start blaming others and pointing your fingers at different departments or other organisations. You have to ask yourself; is this going to benefit the client?

It is at times when things go wrong that people will turn to you for leadership. They will turn to you for guidance and support; so step up, and lead.

You will always be judged on your mistakes. But you will be judged and remembered even more by the way you put things right.

Here's a nice story for you; Paragon Sales Solutions recently conducted a telemarketing campaign for a client. Upon completing the campaign, unfortunately the results were not as good as we would have hoped or wished for. Through no fault of our own; the data was good, and the product that we were trying to market was good. But for whatever reason the campaign just did not generate what should be expected by a client and especially to the standards we work to.

In this moment, I made a decision; I could either hand back the data to the client, shrug my shoulders and explain that things just did not click on this occasion. I could have perhaps made excuses that it was the wrong time of year to sell this kind of offering, and that we were targeting to the wrong audience.

Or, I could plough more hours into the campaign off of my own back and our own costs and try to grab an opportunity for our client.

I chose the latter option. Simply because we always want to deliver strong results and have a strong reputation for delivering quality work. That is one of the reasons we were formed.

Sure, the above scenario might not be considered a mistake as such, however it shows for our willingness to always put things right when things don't necessarily go to plan and when we need to put things right.

The key message I want to portray in this chapter is this; there are always times when things go wrong. There will be times when a delivery is late, there will be times when the quality of your product or service is not as promised. There will also be times when things just do not click as well as they perhaps should.

If any of the above happens; please don't try to hide from it. Don't try to pass blame; it will not do any good. Look to take ownership and ask the question: "What can I do to put it right for you?"

In doing so, you will see that you will an increase in repeat sales, referrals and recommendations; and you will have a whole list of happy customers whom are thankful for the service you have delivered. And that is why you decided to get into business in the first place, right?

Buying Signals

For us all, knowing when to close the sale is crucial. Knowing when the customer is ready to buy could certainly save us an awful lot of time, effort and stress. Not only that; if we try to close the sale at the wrong time it could really put the customer off and can ruin the sale completely!

If you look to close the sale too early and the customer isn't ready to buy, it could really trip you up and leave you looking a little daft. If you try to close the sale after the customer is ready to buy, we could have scared the customer away, turned them off, they could have lost all desire and they might have lost all interest in buying from you.

Therefore it is so important to know when the customer is ready to buy to enhance your chances of actually making the sale.

Now, unless you are Mystic Meg, you won't know exactly when your customer is ready to buy – but there are some clues you can look out for. These are called buying signals. If the customer is ready to buy, they will give you these buying signals which allows you to go in for a test close, or even for a full on close! And do not worry, we will come on to test closing and closing techniques later on in the book.

Let me point out; there are hundreds, if not thousands of buying signals that the people you are selling to will display – and of course each of these will differ from person to person and from scenario to scenario. Unfortunately, we cannot go over all of these right now as we might end up writing a whole new book just dedicated to buying singles and consumer behaviour. However I have noted down four of the biggest signals to look out for. These are by far the most common signals you will see, they are also the easiest to notice and I am certain that at some time during your sales career you will come into contact with at least one of these signals.

If you notice these happen to you during a sales pitch; get ready to close!

Repeating Benefits

What you will notice is that if a customer is really in awe of a benefit of your product or service, they will repeat back to you the benefit in the hope that you validate it for them.

For arguments sake, let's say the phone system that you are selling comes with a two-year guarantee at no extra price, and with only a set-up fee of £100, you may notice your prospect saying;

"So, to confirm, if I sign up, I pay £100 and that includes the two-year guarantee?"

This is your buyer looking to validate the information. Your prospect is just wanting confirmation on these facts. It will also show to you that the points they raise are important to the buyer and must be a key selling point to them. In this buying signal, your prospect will repeat back any of the benefits and values that your product or service brings; so be sure to listen!

If this happens, confirm and validate the information, finish the presentation and go ahead and ask for the sale. There is no point in carrying on the presentation and waffling on about points that might not interest your prospect. So go ahead and close!

Price/Price Plans

Don't worry; if a prospect asks you about price, discounts, or even price plans, it doesn't mean that they are put off or are not interested, and it certainly does not mean they cannot afford your product or service.

In fact, it can be quite the opposite.

It means in their head they can already see the purchase being made – they just now need to confirm pricing. If this happens, be firm, be willing to answer any questions, offer as many payment and pricing options as possible and then look to push the sale forward.

Agreeing

This is a classic non-verbal buying signal and one that is really easy to pick up on.

If you see your prospect nodding along with what you are saying, then the likelihood of it is that they really like what you are pitching and they are ready to buy. If you see this happening a lot during your sales pitch or presentation look to close things up. The last thing you want to do in this situation is to overdo things and bore your prospect to tears.

Yes!

Of course, your prospect agreeing to a sale is a given; a clear and full indication that they want to buy. But if they do verbally say yes, look to do all you can to sign them up, take a deposit, or do anything you can to fully ensure that the sale is closed. Any hesitation from you now can lead to your prospect's desire dropping off or even buyer's remorse further down the line.

As mentioned earlier, there are so many buying signals out there but these four should give you a starting point.

This is why it is so important for you to listen, remain attentive, and be willing to adapt your sales pitch whenever you notice these buying signals.

Developing Rapport

Rapport is a word thrown around a lot in sales. And quite rightly so. If you are not developing a rapport with your prospects and your customers then you will really struggle to influence anyone into buying anything from you.

Remember; relationships within business and sales are crucial to success.

In this chapter I want to share with you a basic understanding of what rapport is, why it is important and I will share with you my five top tips to help you develop rapport with your clients an effective way.

Rapport is simply a strong and positive relationship you have with your prospect, your customer and even the gatekeeper if you work hard enough. Rapport is recognised when you have a lot in common with the person you are communicating with and the communication in general is good and positive.

If you can develop strong rapport with your prospect and your customers then asking for the sale, asking for repeat sales and handling customer relationships all of a sudden become a whole lot easier.

For me, the word rapport is just a little weaker way of saying 'relationship'. You will have heard me say at least a dozen times in this book, and my previous books too most likely, that relationships are the glue that hold sales together. If you can look to develop strong relationships, or rapport, with people then you are really on to a winner and you will be able to find success not just for you, but for your customers too.

Developing rapport with people is easier than you think. In fact, it is no different really to the rapport you develop with people in your social circles. I am sure you are a good enough communicator to be able to spark conversations with people at the pub, the bus stop or even the village fete. Developing rapport with your prospects and your clients and customers is no different at all. Having said all of that, it is your job as a business person, sales professional or entrepreneur to be able to use that rapport and relationship to then push forward with the sale!

If you are looking for new and fresh ideas on how to develop strong rapport with your prospects, these next five tips will certainly help you do just that!

Communicate Well

No one likes being talked to. And no one likes not being listened to. We have covered good communication skills a lot in this book, however it is worth repeating that to develop good rapport with someone you need to communicate well. You need to listen to the person you are talking to, and to actively listen as also. You need to ask questions and understand the answers clearly. You need to use your manners and be polite at all times. It goes without saying; you just need to become a nice person that people love to talk to. Once you become a great communicator and someone that people love to chat to, then you will soon find that people open up to you a lot more and feel more at ease to be able to converse with you.

And doing all of the above will certainly help you with the next tip…

Find Common Ground

We all get on well with people with similar interests and tastes as us. I am sure the majority of your friends and your close ones are people that like similar things to you and have the same views on life. I am sure it is the same with the people you buy from too; you opt for a certain hairdresser because there is common ground, or you always buy a certain brand because you agree with what they stand for.

Whilst communicating with your prospect, try to look for common ground. Look for things that you both like or similar tastes and interests. Once you find these things out, make a note of the things you have in common and be sure to talk about them with your prospect whenever you can.

The common ground you share with your prospect or customer can be anything from watching the same TV Shows, supporting the same football teams or even growing up in the same City.

Whatever it is, communicate and ask your prospect questions to find out the common ground and enjoy a good conversation about it.

Share Experiences

This is an afterburner, or an extension perhaps, from the previous common ground part of the process.

The ability to share an experience is a sure way to solidify a relationship and ensure long term rapport with your prospect. This can be anything from going to a football game or even simply connecting on social media and communicating about non-work activities. Anything you can share with someone will help you to develop long term rapport.

Don't worry about being too pushy or over the top with your approach; if you feel you are pushing the boundaries or being a little too upfront then you most probably are.

But if you feel that there is a little spark there then be sure to go ahead and ask.

Be Empathetic

To be empathetic is the ability to understand and share the feelings of others.

Not everyone you come into contact with is going to have the exact opinions and feelings as you and yet this does not mean you cannot develop rapport with them. By listening to your prospect's views and opinions whilst not taking offence or without judgement will allow you the chance to display a whole new level of caring and will ensure that your rapport is developed. You will gain a lot of respect from your prospect for doing so which in turn will allow for a greater understanding between the two of you. Just because someone has a complete different opinion to you, or a complete different outlook on life to you doesn't mean you cannot do business together.

Mirror

This is such a key thing for me and something that I have written about on countless amounts of times; including in this book already!

The ability to mirror the personality of someone is key to ensuring that you can find common ground and start communicating well. This ensures that you do not come across as someone too loud when you first meet them, or even too shy and quiet. Your ability to match, or mirror, the personality of the person you are speaking with will demonstrate common ground in which you can then develop a strong rapport.

Remember what was said earlier on this book:

"Mirroring is the simple behaviour where you will look to imitate the speech patterns, attitudes, body language and gestures of your prospect. Although this happens often unconsciously and normally goes very unnoticed, by purposefully mirroring your prospect you will see that you will develop strong rapport with people much quicker than normal. You see, when we notice that our actions and gestures are being mirrored then it allows us the chance to feel a higher sense of engagement and belonging within the conversation."

The Test Close

Testing, testing, 123.

We all love a test, right? Well, perhaps not taking tests. No one will ever admit to liking taking tests. But we do love to test things out before we buy. We love to try things out, and ensure that we are making the right decisions; whether it be a trial on Netflix, a test drive or even a trial gym membership.

I remember when I was young, my brother and I built a bridge to an 'island' we found in the fields behind our house. I use the word island quite generously; it was more like a mound of mud no larger than the average garden patio. But, we were young explorers and for all intents and purposes; it was an island! Anyway, after we built the bridge, we knew we needed to test it, to make sure that it would last and not break; allowing us to fall into the murky waters of the brook below. I used to be quite chubby as a kid, and as the heaviest of us, I was volunteered to traverse the bridge first.

"If it can take your weight Rob, it can take everyone else!" my brother exclaimed. So, lo and behold, I started the several meter shuffle to the other side. Well, I wish I could say that our engineering skills were perfect, but that would be a lie. The bridge collapsed just as I got midway, allowing me to drop into the water below. We tested the bridge, or should I say, I tested out the bridge, before we could confirm it was safe.

Before a gig or concert, a band will take part in a sound check so that everyone included can be confident that the sound levels are just right. When you are driving and face a blind T-junction; you don't tend to just shoot out and hope there is no crossing traffic in front of you. You peep, and you creep, until you can see the junction a little clearer and then once safe you can make your way into the junction.

One skill massively overlooked when it comes to sales, is the Test Close. Looking to close more sales? Then the test close could be the tool that is missing from your locker.

Now, if you know me, and know everything I stand for, I am totally against any form of manipulation or pressure tactics to obtain a sale when it just is not right for the prospect. But done in the right way, a test close can ensure that you have answered any relevant questions, made the benefits of your proposal quite clear, and that nothing has been overlooked which will only benefit your prospect and you.

The test close in simple terms is a question you will ask to ensure that you are on the right track with your customer, and to make sure you are explaining everything well and that you are providing enough information. It is also a good way to make sure your customer is still awake! The test close enables you to slow your sales pitch down and to take control of the conversation a little bit more. It will also give you some incredibly vital clues as to how eager the customer is to buy from you.

The kind of question you ask is completely up to you and might differ depending on your prospect. The more you try different options and play around with different test closes the quicker you will find out what works well for you and what does not work so well, but as an idea, any of the following questions could work quite well:

"How do you feel about that?"
"How does that sound?"
"How does that grab you?"

You will see that these questions are open and allow the chance for you to start a conversation with your prospect. These questions are open for a reason; at the test close stage you want to establish that you are answering the right questions and providing the right information for your potential customer. You will still hear either a positive or a negative response, but these give you a chance to engage and converse in the sales pitch. For example:

"How do you feel about that?"

"Yes, it all makes sense so far. But can you just go over the payment terms again?"

or

"How does that sound?"

"Yes, it sounds amazing and exactly what I am looking for!"

The first example gives you clues that you are not quite at the final closing stage just yet. There are still some questions that need to be answered and perhaps some details that you have either missed out, overlooked or did not explain properly. At this stage it will be your job as the advisor to run over those details once again, ensure that your prospect is in full understanding about what you have explained and then go in for another test close statement.

In the second example, it sounds to me like the customer is pretty much ready to buy. Even if at this stage you have some of your proposal or pitch still to go my advice is to just ditch it. Remember what was said in the buying signal chapter of this book; if the buyer is ready to buy then don't over do it. Go in for the close!

There is nothing stopping you trying out a closed question in your test close statement however there are a couple of problems you may face. Do remember that a closed question may come across quite forceful and quite manipulative to your prospect and might push them away or shut them down. If you have not developed a strong enough trust base at this stage with your prospect then you could lose the relationship for good. Also, if you do not get the answer you want, it is very un-natural for you to get the conversation back on track. For example:

"Does that sound good?"

In an ideal world, the prospect may respond; "yes", in which you know you are going in to the closing stage with a high chance of success. But what if you are faced with the response of; "no." The word NO is a massive conversation stopper isn't it? It is a very negative word and you will find that you will be automatically put on the back foot. All of a sudden you will find yourself on the back foot, trying to regain control of your pitch and you face the chance of losing the sale altogether. You and I both do not want that. So perhaps it is best you stick to open questions.

I have coached many sales professionals and one of the questions I have faced on many occasion is:

"Why should I test close? I am a top notch closer. And besides, doesn't the test close just open up another opportunity to be rejected?"

Which are valid points I must admit and perhaps a thought that may have run across my mind on several occasions. Sure, you can go ahead and try to close the sale without a test; but if you have not given enough information, not developed the right level of trust, not quoted the right price or built enough desire then you are only going to get shut down and this final shut down will be the worst of rejection you will face. There could be no coming back from it and you may ultimately lose the sale. Whereas with the test close you are just 'putting it out there'.

You are peeping and creeping towards that all-important sale.

There is a massive chance you have overlooked some details but because of your non-pushy sales technique of just having a conversation with your prospect, you will have a second chance to go over these details once more and to iron out anything you have missed. Think of it as a second chance saloon. From the test close you can then make the decision: "Right, I need to go back to the start of my pitch to answer those questions." Or, "great, I can ditch the rest of my boring pitch and get the ball rolling on having this contract signed!"

A positive response to the test close should bring your desire levels up and enable you to start thinking about the next steps.

A test close needs to be simple - not over complicated. A test close needs to give the prospect the chance to ask any further questions, and should be there to ensure that you can answer those final questions, or perhaps to seal the deal should the buyer be ready to buy!

Ask open ended questions to test close whenever you feel either your buyer looks over excited and ready to buy, or when they look a little lost! You can then either get your pad and paper out and get them to sign should they be ready, or, if they are looking a little puzzled, you can then go over any details you have overlooked and try to sell your product or service again!

So there we are. If you are looking to close more sales, go for the test close! The test close can act as a slight buffer; a way to ensure that you are on to a winner before you try to close the sale and mess up completely!

Understand your Sales Process

Every business needs a sales process. I connect with so many businesses whom do not have a sales process put in place and this can be very damaging for everyone involved. Normally, this is no fault of the business owner whatsoever. There are times when someone will set up a great business idea with no experience of working in sales and so the thought process has never occurred to them.

If you do not have a sales process set up, you needn't worry! At Paragon Sales Solutions setting up sales processes is what we do! Over the years from our own employed life and by working closely with businesses we have become adept and the experts in helping people set up their very own sales processes so that they can see an increase in their sales in a straightforward manner.

Put simply, a sales process is the process that a business owner or sales person will put into place to take a prospect through the early stages of a sale all the way to the closing of the sale. It is pretty much the customers journey and will allow you the chance to know where each of your prospects are in the sales process and the next steps you need to take to look to close the sale. A sales process is in theory a step-by-step guide that you can use as a blueprint that you or any of your team can follow easily.

A sales process could be set out over a week, two weeks, a year or maybe even in just one meeting; this will always depend on what it is you are selling and the prospects you are selling to. The key to you improving your sales is to setting up your own sales process that you can take on board for yourself and even train your team to implement too.

In this chapter I will share with you a basic sales process that you can implement within your business. Do take note however that every business is different, and every sales cycle is different; therefore it is quite hard to take a sales process 'off the shelf' and make it fit. However you can use this as a bit of a guide which you can then fine tune as and when you need to!

In the later examples, always remember that it is very rare for anyone to buy anything from you within the first contact they have with you or your business. In fact, only 2% of all sales are ever made on the first contact; forget what you have seen in 'The Wolf of Wall Street'. I like to work on the basis of there needing to be 5-7 points of contact with a prospect before they sign up or buy from you. And if you utilise this as part of your sales process, it could end up looking a little like this:

Initial Prospecting

This is done at the early stage of the sales process. This can be done either via outgoing prospecting (ie, you as a sales person going out and finding potential customers) or incoming enquiries also. These can all be done face to face, referrals, emails, social media and other marketing and advertising routes. If you are scratching your head thinking of ways in which you can prospect more be sure to head back to the chapter where we covered prospecting in greater deal.
My overall advice is to keep a note of any enquiry, no matter how big or small! If you use a CRM of any shape or form these enquiries, even if they only are a general question, can eventually become a sale if you try to persuade this person down your sales process.

The Relationship Building Phase

It is at this time in which you start to connect with your prospect, develop a rapport and try to discover more about them. This phase in my eyes the most important; fail to set up a strong enough relationship and you can lose the whole sale all together.

You can do this by holding initial conversations, engaging with your prospect and finding that common ground between the two of you. This phase could either take a couple of minutes, or could be spread out over a whole year.

Consultation

The consultation phase is the section of the sales process in which you get the chance to ask your prospect plenty of questions, discover their pain points, and to find the right solution to their problem.

This gives you the chance to solidify the relationship, get to the bottom of your prospects needs and to start coming up with ideas on what to present to them.

Presentation

This is the part of the sales process in which you start to get to the nitty gritty and get the chance to really have your say. You have spent the time to get to know your prospect, you have listened carefully as they have explained exactly what their pain points are and what it is they are looking for from you; it is now your time to prescribe your solution to their problem.

This can be done as a formal presentation, a demonstration, a simple sales pitch or even just a coffee meeting. This gives you the ability to take all of the information passed to you in the earlier stages and then present your ideas.

Ask for the Sale

This can also be known as the closing part of the sale. This is the part in which you finally ask the prospect if they would like to buy your product or service.

The best way for this to happen is for the closing of the sale to be a mutual agreement or understanding that benefits both parties. If you have done all of the earlier stages of your sales process then this should be the easiest part of the sales process. And do not be afraid to take a step or two back up along the process if the prospect has some objections to give to you; this is where the test close really comes in to play.

I always urge my clients to remember that a sale doesn't actually occur until a contact is signed, a deposit is taken or money is exchanged. It can certainly be very tempting to walk away with just a customer's word that they will buy from you but until everything is signed sealed an delivered a sale has not really occurred; so do all you can to get things to the next steps.

How you create your sales process is up to you. There is no real wrong or right way to do it; as long as there is a sales process in place and you and your team know how to operate it then you will see that your sales, and your customers, benefit as a whole.

Managing Expectations

How many times have you been promised the world, but got delivered way under what you expected?

This kind of practice happens so often in sales and can be truly damaging for the reputation and credibility of a business. By over promising and underdelivering you can easily see an increase in 'buyer's remorse' and can also lead to customers not returning to buy from you, and they will also think twice about recommending you to friends and family. You might notice an increase in negative reviews and less people wanting to do business with you.

You might think that a chapter on managing expectations might be quite negative; but by managing your customers expectations you will develop stronger relationships with your prospects and they will learn to trust what you are telling them. It can always be very tempting to just nod your head, agree and go along with whatever your prospect asks in the hope that it encourages them to go ahead with the sale; but this is only a short term fix for a long term problem.

That is why it is so important to manage expectations from the get go and to be truly honest about what will be delivered to the customer and to what time scale.

Honesty always prevails. You will soon find that in managing your customers' expectations and giving them a full breakdown as to what they will expect you will receive their utmost trust; respect and you will develop a strong relationship with them that will last far longer than if you were to over-promise.

I am a firm believer that good sales is just a further extension of great customer service – serve your customers honestly and fully, and your will see a huge increase in your sales over the long-term.

This is also why I always encourage sales people to not be worried about saying no from time to time.

Do you sometimes feel like you are a 'yes man'? Constantly agreeing to the customers' demands and saying **YES** to everything they ask and demand?

Then stop!

Of course, it can be really tempting to say yes to everything the customer asks for but what happens in the long run if you agree to something that you simply cannot offer, or if you have no experience in that offering? Over time you are only going to ruin customer confidence and destroy your businesses reputation.

The same can be said when it comes to price reductions or discounts. Are you offering too many discounts on your products or services because you are scared of saying no? Not only can this damage your profit margins but can also devalue your product or service and can really harm your credibility.

So next time you feel you want to say yes, and to agree to every single one of your customers' demands ask yourself this; will I be able to keep up with what it is I am offering? Will you end up devaluing or harming your product, your service, or your business.

You really do not want to be seen as just a 'yes man'. You want to be seen as someone whom is respected by your customer and someone who will work hard to develop a long-lasting business relationship with them – which in turn will help you to see a higher return in sales.

Hitting Your Sales Target

I work closely with a lot of sales teams, and sales professionals from all around the world to help them to increase their sales.

Whenever I take on a sales training client, or deliver a sales training course, I like to sit down with my clients to understand their needs and to ensure that I can deliver the right possible course that will help them to see an increase in their sales and ultimately their profits.

One thing that I see an awful lot of is sales people not truly understanding, or taking the time, to work out the key parts to their role that they need to do to ensure overall success.

One key example of this is not breaking down their sales targets.

Sales targets dominate sales rooms everywhere you go. Sales targets are there to keep us focused, to keep us on track, and to give us something to aim for. But for some, they can become daunting, and become a figure that they just hope they get. They just 'hit and hope' and allow for a bit of guess work to get there.

These sales targets might have been set to you by your management, your business partner or just set by yourself; either way, it is so important that there is some form of target in place to work towards and to try to achieve.

As mentioned earlier, there is one simple thing that you can do to ensure you always hit your target.

Break it down!

So, for this example let's keep it simple. Your sales target is £100 – sounds easy enough right? At this stage you can take two roads; either just go about your daily routine and hope you make the target, or you can set up a structure to help you reach it; effectively breaking the target down.

The sales target in this example is £100, and your average selling price is £10 – so you know you need to make ten sales.

However, it is never that simple. To make the sale, you know that you need to meet people face to face. On average, your conversion rate is that 1 in every 4 meetings ends in a sale. Therefore, statistically speaking, you need to meet with 40 prospects to make the 10 sales you need to hit target.

But it doesn't stop there. You know from experience that you need to call 5 prospects to get you 1 appointment. Therefore, you need to be calling 200 prospects, which will set you up with the 40 meetings you need, to get you the 10 sales.

Does all of that make sense?

Of course there is never such an exact science to these things but if you pay attention and start to test and take notes on your performance you will soon start to see a pattern emerging that will help you to set true, real targets.

So with this above example, you now know that you need to target yourself with 200 calls, or maybe 20 calls a day which will then feed your sales pipeline adequately to give you enough of a chance to close enough sales to meet your target.

By breaking down your sales goals gives you the chance to truly understand where you as a sales professional or business owner need to allocate your time. It is only in this way that you can ensure time after time you are going to smash any sales target set out in front of you.

So whether you have set your own sales target, or someone has set you a target, don't ever feel daunted by it. A sales target is put in place to give you something to aim for and to give you something to work towards; but by breaking it down you are given the steps to success that you can simply follow just one step at a time.

Don't Close the Sale!

We are led to believe that a sales process should be fast and rushed through with little regard for the finer detail. There are many out there whom will rush a transaction through in the hope of hitting a target, either a personal one or perhaps even a management led target, or will rush the sale through to earn some quick money.

We have all been there and this is in no way an individual fault. It is a way of business which has dominated our whole entire sales forces up and down the country from antiques dealers right up to car sales people - our minds have been focussed far too greatly on the small sale. The one hit transaction. The quick turnaround. The closing of the sale.

But have you ever set your sights on the long term?

The difference between a good sales person, and a GREAT sales professional is the ability to think of the bigger picture.

The fact of the matter is this; we can all 'sell'. We have all negotiated with someone in our personal lives to get something from life we want. It could be persuading your group of friends to try your favourite bar and to divulge in their new 'Happy Hour' cocktail menu, or it could perhaps be selling your children the idea of an earlier bed time (yes that is right, these two examples are sales transactions! So don't ever let me hear you say you are not a sales person! We all are!)

Selling one off ideas such as these however doesn't turn you into a great sales professional. What will stand you apart in your quest for business success will be your passion for ensuring your customer has walked away from the transaction with everything that they could have possibly desired in a friendly and straight forward manner; and they will be more than happy to come back to you time and time again.

A great sales professional will not rush things, and yet will keep the process as concise as possible (we all hate time wasters, right?) A great sales professional will listen with good intent to their prospect and do all that they can to answer every single question that he or she may have - we were born with two ears for a reason!

To ensure your business grows, and to build the foundations of a great sales force you must lead by example and truly care for your customer. By truly caring you will not just close every transaction that comes your way; you will also be swamped with recommendations, referrals and even repeat customers some would call that the Three R's of Selling.

These Three R's of Selling are three of the most important things you should rely on to ensure you keep selling time after time and that your business thrives. These Three R's will not happen if you are just looking to constantly close sales after sale without any desire to develop relationships or to take care of your customer; and yet if you can develop relationships these three things will help you to keep hitting your sales targets.

Recommendations

You want to be the first person on anyones lips for when they need to recommend someone.

We see it all the time; a neighbour, friend or even a Facebook contact will be seeking out recommendations for a certain product or service.

If you do not give your customers and clients a good and positive experience you will never be recommended. You will become forgotten and will have less enquiries coming towards you.

Referrals

As we discussed earlier on this book, referrals are one of the best ways you can prospect and if done correctly will allow you the chance to fill up your sales pipeline full of prospects that will have a good foundation of trust within you.

Your customer will not be willing to refer you to their friends or families if you have not supported or looked after them that well. But by taking care of your customers and supporting them, even after the sale has occurred, your customer will be more willing to refer you people to talk to.

Repeat Business

If you can make fans out of your customers, and have them coming back to you time and time again you will not only save a lot of time and effort in your sales process but you could also save a large chunk of your marketing budget.

People will only buy from you again if their experience first time around was the best possible.

You must be willing to be at the end of the telephone for your customer and be willing to be there to support, assist and even act as a consultant at times for your customer as they go through the sales process. We live in an age where every customer can shop around and seek advice from unlimited links on the internet - so don't take your customer for granted. Be the advisor you wish you had every time you had to make a big purchase. And a lot of this advice I am talking about needs to be taken into account even after the transaction has been completed.

So before you go ahead and close the sale, remember this; in closing the sale, you are in fact opening up a relationship that you will need to put a lot of effort into. A bad sales person will close the sale, and the relationship alongside it. If you are willing to work hard and make the effort, you will be rewarded with the Three R's of Selling - do you see what I did there?

I will end this chapter with the one quote which really changed my outlook on sales quite early on in my career; "People like to buy, but they hate to be sold".

Don't just close a sale to hit a target, or to tick another box for your reports. Close a sale to open up a relationship. And make it profitable for both parties. It's a two way thing.

If you can do all of that, you will soon be on your way to becoming a great sales professional and a very successful business owner.

Closing the Sale

Closing a sale is near enough the best result you aim for when creating your sales process (although the hard work has only just begun). The closing stage is the section of the process in which all of your creativity, prospecting, questioning and overcoming objections has brought you to. This is the section you finally reach out and close the sale, or to put it in a more physical term: this is the section you get pen to paper and have your prospect sign your order form.

Closing the sale is just you asking for the sale!

Don't be misled; this chapter will not teach you manipulative techniques to push your prospect over the line nor will it give you clues on how to use emotional blackmail to get the end result that you are after. You will have read already in this book, and also within Relationship Selling and The Paragon Mindset that I am strongly against selling for the sake of selling or to sell to just hit a target.

What I do stand strongly for however is finding solutions to problems and assisting your buyer in finding the right match for their needs. That being said, the closing stage of the sale is important. Think of it like this; let's say you want to grow some tomatoes in your garden. You go out to various shops looking for the right seeds, along with the right compost and the right tools. You get the equipment home and after some research on the right area of the garden to plant the seeds, you go ahead and get them in the compost. With the seeds planted, you wait. From time to time you water them, feed them, until eventually the seedling shoots from the ground and the tiny green plant shows its face. That's not the end part though. You watch the plant grow and grow and as it does you continue to water it, feed it and you support its long shoots with trellis and twine. Eventually, after a lot of love and care the first flowers start to show. These flowers eventually turn into beautiful red tomatoes, just ready to be eaten. But what if you were to leave that fruit on the vines? They would sit there waiting for you to pick them, waiting for you to enjoy them and yet you never do. Over time the tomatoes become rotten, the fruit falls to the ground and returns back to the soil. Or someone else comes along and takes the fruit that you have so beautifully nurtured.

This parable relates to a sales process where the sales person forgets to close it. You have prospected well by sourcing the customer and finding out their needs. You have planted the seed by telling them how you can help them and what you can provide to them. Over time and nurturing, your prospect is ready to buy. They give off buying signals and display to you that they want to buy - they display their tomatoes! However, you neglect to close the sale. You don't allow your customer the opportunity to buy and eventually the relationship and sales cycle has run its course. The opportunity has passed and you either have to start all over again; either with your current prospect or by going out and finding a new prospect. I know from experience that if you miss your first opportunity to ask for the sale it is very hard to come back from that. It highlights once again the need for trust. If your prospect has no faith in you to get the deal signed and put the ball in motion, then for them to trust you to do it again is a hard thing to regain.

Therefore, you can see why it is important to get that sale closed. In this chapter I want to share with you some theories behind closing techniques, some good practices that you should take on board for your careers, and also ideas on how you can increase your chances to get the sale!

I want to start with attitude. Many people are very scared to ask for the sale. Once upon a time I too was scared to close a sale. This simply stems down to a fear of rejection, a fear of damaging a relationship, and in some cases, a need to be liked. For many, closing the sale can be a very worrying moment in the sales cycle - they may be really good at questioning, prospecting and developing a relationship, however, when it comes to actually close the sale, they lose their confidence. This is a completely natural thing and if this relates to you then there is nothing to be ashamed of, embarrassed of or concerned about. The bad news I have to share with you is that the more you practice closing, the better you become. So there really is no hiding from it! I don't want to talk too much about rejection just yet as there will be a section of this book later on dedicated to rejection, how to handle it and how to overcome it, however, I need to warn you that you will get rejected from time to time. Not every sales pitch or presentation is going to end in a sale - so do not put too much pressure on yourself and do not fear rejection. Shake it off, learn from it, and move on to your next customer.

It can be very easy to get stuck into a mindset attitude of thinking that you are going to be rejected way before you have stepped into a meeting, especially if you are on a streak of rejection and you have not made a sale in a while. It can be easy to get in the habit of assuming that you will be turned down and this can be very detrimental to your selling efforts. No matter what kind of streak you are going through or what results you have had recently, it is vitally important that on every sales call, in every meeting and every pitch you assume you will make the sale. It is this positive and strong mental attitude that will help you to not only build resilience but will also help you to get the sale. No one wants a grumpy sales person trying to talk to them and trying to offer them a product or a service. It will just not work out at all. In your sales preparation, be sure to stand up tall, smile, and picture yourself walking away with that sale at the end of the sales call. I have seen and witnessed countless sales professionals all of whom after a long run of rejection will just pick up the phone and 'go through the motions'. They don't care what the outcome of the call will be, and they are just doing so either in routine, or to just finish their call list. I have been there too - it feels like a big heavy NO sign is sitting on your shoulders and is weighing you down. I guarantee to you that you will get more sales if you forget what ever has gone on in previous sales meetings, you forget what happened on your last sales call and you treat this call like it is your first, you treat it like you have a written assurance that the customer is going to sign up whilst you are there. This can take a lot of work to get right and take a lot of practice, but it is vital you reset the score sheet before your next call. The right winning mental attitude will certainly get you the result you want if utilised in the right way.

Remember, people buy for their reasons, not yours.

Trying to close a sale because it will help you to hit your sales target, to impress your boss, or to ensure the business has a quick injection of cash will not work. If you are at this stage and you have had the right conversations with your prospect or customer, then there should be a certain chance that you have asked them the right questions to get you to this stage. You have asked them about their 'weakness' their 'problems' and got to the bottom of what it is they are looking for. You should now simply be willing to ask the customer for the sale or be willing to ask them if they are ready to buy. You are already pre-armed with some objections that you are going to potentially face along with appropriate responses, so you are now fully ready to listen to the rejection and try to find a way through it.

I have seen countless sales people assume they can only make the closing question at the end of their presentation or pitch. This is a big, big mistake. As we just discussed, people buy for their reasons. People will buy when their desire for your product or your service is at the highest point. Think of it like a time line running horizontally from left to right. As the presentation goes on and you ask the right questions the buyers desire will rise, like the incline of a roller coaster. If you keep talking, keep presenting and keep waffling on, over time this desire is then going to drop off back down to its starting point and the desire will be gone. They could be bored, fed up, ready for a coffee or just thinking ahead to their next meeting. If you were to end your presentation here and then ask for the sale, what do you think is going to happen? Whereas if you were to ask a closing question when your buyers desire is at the highest and when they are pretty much sitting on the edge of the seat ready to put pen to paper, guess what is going to happen then? Yes, you guessed it - the chances of the sale are going to be pretty high.

Don't forget to try out a test close if you feel you need a buffer to protect you and to protect your prospect. If they are ready to buy; go ahead and ask for the sale.

Following on from the 'test close', the final close needs to match the test close and continue on a path to get the deal signed and the product or service delivered. In fact, the test close can in theory become the final closing statement if the customer is ready to buy. For example:

"How do you feel about that Mrs Prospect?"

"Yes, that all looks great to me!"

"Fantastic. Why don't we go over the finer details and look to get this product out to you by next week?"

Or

"How does that sound?"

"Yes, that sounds fantastic. Just what I was looking for."

"Fantastic! Let's get the ball rolling then so we can start servicing you from Wednesday!"

As you can see, the test close does a lot of the hard work for you so all you have to do is finish off the conversation and put pen to paper on the deal you have been working so damn hard for.

It is very important I must add that whenever looking to close the sale you give full eye contact throughout. Eye contact develops trust and allows your prospect the chance to develop faith in what you are saying and understand that you are not going to let them down.

Do not allow tedious paperwork or regulations to get in the way of a sale either. I have seen it first hand; you could be selling a really good service, and yet when your prospect agrees to sign up, the paperwork puts them off. It could be long winded, complicated and full of jargon that makes no sense. If you have any say in your own application forms or order forms, then make them as streamlined and accessible as possible. Do not over complicate them for the sake of it or to look more professional than you are. You will only look more foolish! Keep your paperwork as plain as possible. If you do not have a say over your order forms or application forms, then do what you can to help your applicant fill them out. Perhaps just leave an 'X' next to the personal information that they need to complete themselves, and allow yourself time back at the office to fill out the basic stuff such as their name, address etc. Once again, your prospect will thank you later for saving them this headache!

Do not forget, and never be under any illusion the sale is never truly complete until all financial transactions are completed, and goods or services are delivered. So once any contract is signed or any final proposals are delivered, do not celebrate early and forget why you were working so hard in the first place! Your customer! Your customer is the reason you are about to celebrate so thank them and remain professional and supportive throughout the next transitional phase. A sale can and on so many occasions has been lost after the final close. This can be due to 'buyer's remorse'. Perhaps a feeling of guilt, regret, or second thoughts. Perhaps the customer can suddenly find out more about you and your company or the way you work and start to distrust you. All of these things can be avoided with good relationship development which as mentioned before will be brought up later on in the book but at the very least - thank the customer. Right then and there. Thank them and make a promise that you will deliver everything you have pledged to deliver. Do not let your customer down at this stage!

Your Next Steps

The past couple of hundreds of pages should have given you enough inspiration, advice and ideas on how you can increase your sales. I have ensured I have included something for everyone in this book; from the complete sales beginners all the way up to the seasoned professionals.

One thing is really important moving forward however; if you do not put these chapters into practice then you will not see an increase in your sales.

You see, the words written within this book are not just invented from my own imagination. They have come from years of studying, practice, success and failures. The reading of this book is just the start.

Sales skills are only ever developed by a mixture of studying, which you have just done, and practice. It is now your time to get out there and to sell more!

If you want to continue to learn and to enhance your sales skills however there are a couple of options for you. You could read this book over again, perhaps making notes and highlighting the key aspects that really appeal to you. You can read my other books, Relationship Selling or The Paragon Mindset; both of which are still available to buy in paperback and Kindle from amazon.co.uk. You can find our YouTube channel and watch our hundreds of free sales training videos, or you can log into our new website:

improveyoursales.co.uk

This website is host to plenty of useful sales tools, guides, videos and courses to help you improve your sales.

Do be sure to leave a glowing review for this book on Amazon and recommend it to your colleagues, peers and friends!

Above everything mentioned within this book, remember one thing; you are in full control of your sales and your business.

If you want to improve your sales and to see an increase in your sales then only you have the power to do so. Reading this book, and looking at my other materials will certainly be a good start and will give you the tools to do so; but only you can implement these things.

Get yourself out there. Prospect well. Develop strong relationships. And always look to take the next steps.

Until next time,

Robert Spence

improveyoursales.co.uk

Other Works by Robert Spence

Relationship Selling

Relationship Selling: Achieve Everything You Deserve is the best-selling sales guide written by Robert Spence.

His first book has earned rave reviews on Amazon from readers all around the world and is highly regarded as a highly motivational book by business people, sales professionals and entrepreneurs.

We are all Sales People. No matter what line of work you are in, you are a sales person. Every single day you will need to sell yourself and convince others you deserve to be treated better. Whether you are going for a job interview, asking for a pay rise from your boss or even going on a romantic date; you have to persuade others to give you what you truly deserve. Relationship Selling is a straight-talking guide on how to become a better you, how to increase your sales, how to build and develop strong business and personal relationships and how to get more from each and every single day. You have two choices; either carry on dreaming about a greater career whilst wishing for the finer things in life. Or, you can work hard, set yourself the goals needed to strive for better and to achieve everything you deserve. Relationship Selling dives head first into the most profitable sales techniques used by millions of sales professionals around the globe, allowing you the chance to learn what it takes to increase your commission cheque month after month.

Other Works by Robert Spence

The Paragon Mindset

The Paragon Mindset is Robert Spence's second sales guide and has gone on to sell copies worldwide and has become the go-to guide for sales professionals everywhere!

With five star reviews on Amazon, this book is a must for any sales professional, business owner or entrepreneur.

Attitude, belief and mindset are all attributes that separate the average sales people from the elite. Having a strong sales team is what separates a surviving enterprise from a thriving business. No matter your current approach to sales, The Paragon Mindset is the book that will help you to not only sell more, but will also help you to achieve more. Filled with solid advice, techniques and sales boosting skill sets, The Paragon Mindset is the book to help you to increase your sales.

Printed in Dunstable, United Kingdom